Praise for *The Telling*

"Here is Gerson's inimitable voice—passionate, erudite, and most of all deeply in love with Jewish wisdom. Read this book to understand why the Haggadah has endured as a seminal Jewish text and why it remains no less relevant today than when it was first written."

—Yossi Klein Halevi, author of *Letters to My Palestinian Neighbor* and *Like Dreamers*

"*The Telling* is absolutely fascinating—so insightful, so brilliantly written, so informative. I learned so much, and love the perspective." —Paul Osteen, Lakewood Church

"Mark Gerson's *The Telling* is as broadly creative and inclusive as it is rigorous and intellectually deep. This book will reach, engage, and inspire countless people whose families and communities will discover new meaning and purpose through the book's myriad insights."

—Rabbi Jonah Pesner, director of the Religious Action Center of Reform Judaism

"I'm no expert on Jewish worship. I'm not even Jewish. But this deep and wise book moved me. Mark Gerson has a remarkable talent for unearthing new insights in ancient stories."

—Tucker Carlson, host of *Tucker Carlson Tonight*

"Transformative and compelling, Mark Gerson's inspired book *The Telling* brings us into the Haggadah as a guide for life, given to the Jewish people, but a gift for all humanity. The ideas in this captivating book will enable everyone to enjoy lives that are fuller and richer."

—Bishop Robert Stearns, pastor at the Full Gospel Tabernacle and founder and executive director of Eagles' Wings

"In *The Telling*, Mark Gerson brilliantly illuminates some of the big questions from the Haggadah whose answers can define what constitutes a meaningful life. By showing how the Haggadah enables its readers to deploy ancient Jewish wisdom to help answer the most contemporary questions, this book will help your Pesach to be what it can be: a life-guiding event, every year, for anyone who learns enough to give it the opportunity."

—Senator Joseph Lieberman

"With a broad range of sources, deep insight, and true wisdom, Mark Gerson renews for his readers the enchantment of the Passover celebration."

—Rabbi David Wolpe, Sinai Temple, Los Angeles

The Telling is the perfect introduction for those desiring to explore this aspect of Jewish life. This book is full of knowledge and thought-provoking questions and answers to the many mysteries that surround this sacred Jewish holiday."

—Tiki Barber, former running back for the New York Giants, radio host at CBS Sports Radio, and former cast member of *Kinky Boots* on Broadway

"In *The Telling*, Mark Gerson gives a masterful overview of the principles underlying the Seder. For anyone looking to explore purpose in a modern world, and anyone looking to add lively discussion to your next observance of Pesach, this book is for you."

—Gordon Robertson, CEO of the Christian Broadcasting Network

"*The Telling* is dynamic, accessible, inclusive, and effervescent. Mark Gerson's wise teachings make the Haggadah relevant in any contemporary context. Religious Jews, cultural Jews, unaffiliated Jews, non-Jews—if you have a curious mind and thirst for knowledge, this book will enrich your life and enhance your world."

—Amanda Berman, founder and executive director of Zioness Movement

"Just when I thought I knew everything about the Haggadah, I opened up Mark Gerson's book, and sure enough, I found myself thinking differently, questioning, and wrestling with big new ideas. I am excited to bring these ideas forward to my family's Seder and meaningful conversations all year round." —Sarah Waxman, founder of At The Well

"Mark Gerson teaches us that the Almighty has given us two guidebooks for life: the Torah and the Haggadah. In *The Telling*, we learn much more than Passover customs, making the book far more profound and useful: loving the stranger, the source of antisemitism, the secret to happiness and goodness, becoming a better person, and when bad things happen to good people. Learn master tactics from Moses, raise better kids, and inspire others to improve. Read this to gain new spirit, new insight, and new intuition on Judaism and life. Really." —Dr. Rick Hodes, medical director of JDC's Ethiopia Spine and Heart project

"Mark Gerson draws on a diverse set of Jewish and secular wisdom to illuminate the Passover story in all its boundless depth. This book, which seamlessly transitions between rich story-telling, fascinating Biblical interpretation, and deep historical context, is another reminder of why the Haggadah has been treasured by Jews for thousands of years. *The Telling* is a vital contribution to the Seder—it's a guide to the great Jewish guidebook."

—Dan Senor, author of *Start-Up Nation*

"*The Telling* makes very audacious statements, asks provocative questions, teaches some of the greatest Torah, and yet at the same time provides simple wisdom . . . all in one book!"

—Rabbi Sherre Hirsch, chief innovation officer at American Jewish University and author of *Thresholds: How to Thrive Through Life's Transitions to Live Fearlessly and Regret-Free*

"The Jewish people have a powerful message from God to share about being delivered from a life of slavery and brought into God's purpose for them as a nation. In his book *The Telling*, Mark Gerson helps us understand so much about the importance of the Passover and how it impacts our lives today as Christians. When Jews and Christians come together around this sacred biblical text, I believe that historic things will take place."

—A. R. Bernard, pastor of Christian Cultural Center Megachurch

"As believers, there is so much we can gain from the story of the Exodus Passover, when God brought the children of Israel out of bondage by His mighty hand. With the powerful book *The Telling* by Mark Gerson, you will learn from a Hebrew perspective many hidden aspects of the Passover story that will bless your life. Get ready to encounter the God of the miraculous like you never have before!" —Judy Shaw, Judy Shaw Ministries

" . . . an invaluable resource for all those who crave new material for family celebrations . . . Though the book is certainly learned . . . it is not written for insiders . . . Because the book packs so much into every page, one leaves the experience of reading it with a desire to one day return. The book is a quick, but compelling read, with the option to go slow and take in all the information Gerson doles out."

—Rabbi Marc Katz, author of *The Heart of Loneliness: How Jewish Wisdom Can Help You Cope and Find Comfort*

"This beautifully written book is a fascinating guide for living a meaningful life. I highly recommend it." —Jon Gordon, author of *The Energy Bus: 10 Rules to Fuel Your Life, Work, and Team with Positive Energy*

"When trumpets were mellow // And every gal only had one fellow // No need to remember when // 'Cause everything old is new again." Peter Allen and Carole Singer could have been singing about Mark Gerson, who breathes new life into ancient tradition in *The Telling*. With wit, wisdom, and scholarly erudition, Gerson draws inspiring and moving lessons from the rituals and stories of Passover. *The Telling* is manna for your mind and heart." —Safi Bahcall, author of *Loonshots*

"As a Gentile, I had read in the book of Exodus many times concerning the Passover. I now read it from a different viewpoint after reading Mark Gerson's *The Telling*. The Passover and the parting of the Red Sea tell us of the freeing of the children of Israel from Pharaoh and the Egyptians. As focused in *The Telling*, the Passover was so much more than just freeing the Jews. The Passover told the whole world, then and now, the power of God. I encourage other Gentiles to read *The Telling* to gain further focus into the awesome power our God showed the whole world with His tenth plague against Egypt." —Dr. Richard Furman, founder of World Medical Mission

"In his book about a book, Gerson weaves these strands together masterfully . . . He brings life and relevance to seemingly arcane passages, providing insights capable of enlightening and enlivening any seder—from the deeply traditional to the generically spiritual and political." —Bruce Abramson, director of the American Center for Education and Knowledge, author of *The New Civil War: Exposing Elites, Fighting Utopian Leftism, and Restoring America*

"*The Telling* . . . is different from every other book about Passover, Judaism, and yes, the meaning of life . . . Gerson is at once thoroughly Jewish and quintessentially American. He ends on this note: 'Pesach, like everything else meaningfully Jewish, is never finished.' Like everything American. In fact, like everything human. *L'Chaim*." —Juliana Geran Pilon, author of *The Utopian Conceit and the War on Freedom*

THE
TELLING
Workbook

ALSO BY MARK GERSON

The Telling

THE TELLING Workbook

An Interactive Guide to the Haggadah

MARK GERSON

ST. MARTIN'S
ESSENTIALS

NEW YORK

First published in the United States by St. Martin's Essentials, an imprint of St. Martin's Publishing Group

THE TELLING WORKBOOK. Copyright © 2022 by Mark Gerson. All rights reserved. Printed in the United States of America. For information, address St. Martin's Publishing Group, 120 Broadway, New York, NY 10271.

www.stmartins.com

Designed by Steven Seighman

The Library of Congress Cataloging-in-Publication Data is available upon request.

ISBN 978-1-250-84318-0 (trade paperback)
ISBN 978-1-250-84319-7 (ebook)

Our books may be purchased in bulk for promotional, educational, or business use. Please contact your local bookseller or the Macmillan Corporate and Premium Sales Department at 1-800-221-7945, extension 5442, or by email at MacmillanSpecialMarkets@macmillan.com.

First Edition: 2022

10 9 8 7 6 5 4 3 2 1

CONTENTS

INTRODUCTION

The Telling was published a year ago, in time for Pesach preparation 2021. It will be remembered, perhaps, as the liminal Pesach—the Pesach that existed between Pesach '20, whose celebration was overshadowed and defined by the COVID-19 pandemic, and Pesach '22, which will (one hopes) be celebrated in a manner more common to years past. The long-term impact of COVID-19 on our celebrations of Pesach will, like so many things related to the pandemic, be known only in the fullness of time.

I can speak confidently only of the impact of the liminal Pesach on *The Telling*. Long before I knew that I was doing so, I began studying the texts and ideas that would become the basis for *The Telling*. The process began around fifteen years ago, when I discovered that the Haggadah really was the Greatest Hits of Jewish Thought, curated magnificently to enable us to experience the Jewish New Year (which is what Pesach is). Why magnificently? Because the Haggadah is the most interesting, instructive, sustaining, and simply true self-help book ever written. It harnesses the entire corpus of Jewish learning in order to help us lead happier, more fulfilling, and more meaningful lives.

I wrote *The Telling* in order to show how the Maggid section of the Haggadah, through its many passages (most of which are familiar to almost every Jew), accomplishes this by guiding us in our decisions and our character, in our relationships and our ideas—in the most highly practical and immediately actionable ways.

My book tour began in early March '21, upon publication of *The Telling* four weeks ahead of the Seder. Because of COVID, the book tour was conducted entirely online. This proved to be a blessing. I was able to do up to five events a day, speaking to groups around the world, all within a several-hour period. These events, which were usually with churches or synagogues, enabled me to speak to, take questions, and receive comments from thousands of people who had read or were soon to read at least part of the book.

The new ways to introduce the book to its intended audience, from podcasts to social media, enabled even greater connectivity to readers.

The response was deeply gratifying, in multiple ways. The book made bestseller lists from the *LA Times* to *Publishers Weekly*. It received critical acclaim in secular and religious publications. I received many emails from pastors and rabbis inviting me into discussion with them about the Pesach holiday, and was thus able to discuss the Exodus story with so many more people.

And I received a lot of emails and other communications from readers. These readers sent me outlines of the Seders they planned to conduct that were based on the book, reports of questions and answers aroused at the Seder by *The Telling*, and commitments that they made based on ideas derived from the book.

Many of these readers came to me with similar suggestions for what would make the book even more useful to them. They said (some directly and some by inference) that there should be a *Telling* workbook, a workbook that Seder attendees could use to prompt thought, stimulate discussion, and make commitments.

I deeply appreciated everything about this idea, as it would help drive home the mission of *The Telling*—to make this greatest of holidays what it can, should, and was always intended to be: the moral driver of the Jewish year, in the most practical, existential, and interesting ways. And I never would have thought of doing a workbook without the suggestions of these readers. I didn't even know what a workbook was before they suggested it.

So: I am delighted that this book has ended up in your hands! How is it best used? A student once approached the great nineteenth-century rabbi the Kotzker Rebbe and told him that he had been through the Talmud three times. The Kotzker Rebbe effectively replied, "How many times has the Talmud been through you?"

Similarly, one can go through the entire Haggadah on Seder night. But there is simply not enough time on Seder night to go through the entire Haggadah (or anything close to it) with the kind of probing, enlightening, serendipitous, and existential discussion that a genuine experience of this holiday enables. This philosophy is embodied in the workbook.

Both *The Telling* and *The Telling Workbook* have many chapters, each corresponding to a familiar passage in the Haggadah. Readers/users should identify the three to seven chapters that are most meaningful to them and their guests at the Seder. Focus on them, necessarily to the exclusion of others. A wonderful use of this book would be to, on or before Seder night, have guests consider the passages in the selected chapters and answer just some of the questions in the workbook—thoughtfully, rigorously, meaningfully. Will this leave a lot of interesting, valuable, and fulfilling passages undiscovered? Yes. As discussed in the chapter "The Unfinished" in *The Telling,* the hallmark of a Jewish story or a Jewish experience is that it concludes unfinished. At the same time, this workbook contains a lot of blank space. This blank space is meant to invite you, the reader, to engage with the questions, to write your answers directly on the page, and perhaps to see how your answers change from year to year.

My appreciation here is deeply felt, but not limited to, the readers who led me to this workbook. I would also like to extend my great appreciation to Phil Getz, who epitomizes what it means to be a great editor. His intimacy with the subject and his concern for everything from ideas to punctuation—which presented in his creativity, his originality, his structuring of sentences, and so much more—helped make this book (and *The Telling* itself) what they are.

I would also like to thank my chief of staff, Daniel Jeydel, for great work in (among other things!) making sure that *The Telling* promotion process went so smoothly last year . . . which led to this book.

I would also like to thank Bishop Robert Stearns and his colleagues at their remarkable organization Eagles' Wings. Eagles' Wings arranged for dozens of talks I gave to churches— all in service of one of their great goals: Jewish-Christian understanding, appreciation, friendship, and indeed love through a shared affection for all things Jewish: the Jewish state, Jewish practices, and Jewish study and teaching. The Christians who attended these events had such enthusiasm for the important ideas about Pesach and the Exodus that I started doing these events with another screen open—to take notes of insights I learned from them to include in the next edition of the book.

And I would like to thank Joel Fotinos, the publisher at St. Martin's Essentials. He and his team were a pleasure to work with on *The Telling*—and what a pleasant surprise to discover that Joel is also the master of the workbook genre. (His workbook on Napoleon Hill's *Think and Grow Rich* is a classic.)

And, of course, I would like to thank my wife, Rabbi Erica Gerson—for, among other things, making my life a Torah workbook.

Next year in Graceland!

THE REAL JEWISH NEW YEAR

Pesach, the Torah tells us, shall occur at "the head of months." It is, therefore, as *The Telling* explains (p. 7), the authentic Jewish New Year. And it is no coincidence that the Torah instructs that it is to occur "in the month of spring." Every culture has a spring festival. There is Holi in northern India, the Songkran Water Festival in Thailand, the Festival of Scrambled Eggs in Bosnia, Opening Day in the United States—and Pesach in Judaism.

Why does every culture have a spring festival? Because of the universal feeling evoked by the season. We feel renewed and rejuvenated. We go outside again and feel the sense of opportunity and newness in the air.

However, this poses a logistical problem for Judaism's lunar calendar. Any day on a lunar calendar will, after enough time, rotate through the years. For instance, the Muslim holy month of Ramadan has occurred in every season.

How, then, could a Jewish holiday on a lunar calendar be affixed to a season?

Pesach is so important in Jewish life that in order to make our New Year coincide with spring, we add a leap month in seven out of every nineteen years.

Why do we go to such lengths to ensure that Pesach, our New Year, always occurs in the spring?

In Judaism, the spiritual and the physical are never separate. When we welcome the Sabbath every week, we say, "Wake up, wake up / For your light has come: rise, shine! Awake, Awake, break out in song / For the Lord's glory is revealed on you." This is of course a spiritual awakening with a physical expression because the two are intertwined. We always aspire for them to complement each other. Consequently, we celebrate our New Year when we feel renewed, rejuvenated—and ready to take stock of who we are now, contemplate who we might be in the coming year, and make the commitments and resolutions necessary to become that person.

This is all done in the spirit of spring.

1. In what specific ways do you want to change in the coming year? What characteristics do you want to develop in order to be a different—and better—person?

2. What resolutions are you prepared to make *today* in order to achieve those goals?

> Not many people realize that the Exodus story is . . .
> the foundation of the modern world.
>
> —VISHAL MANGALWADI

HAGGADAH: WHEN A GREAT BOOK IS NOT MEANT TO BE READ

In Exodus 13:8, Moses issues the instruction that birthed the Seder: "You shall tell your son on that day, 'It is because of what the Lord did for me when I came out of Egypt.'"

The obligation is thus to "tell." There are many ways to tell a story. Yet we chose to do so by commissioning a book. That book is called the Haggadah—and *Haggadah* means "telling."

The first question to ask about any book is: What is its genre? As explained in *The Telling* (p. 13), the Haggadah is not a cookbook or a lawbook, an instruction manual or a dinner program, that we muddle through and tolerate en route to the meal. The Haggadah, like the Torah from which it derives, exists (per Deuteronomy 10:3) "for your benefit." It is a guidebook—a guidebook for life.

But we don't read, or *just* read, this guidebook. We experience it. Specifically, we use the Haggadah to "retell" and "relive" the story of the Exodus. And we have been doing it for thousands of years in every corner of the world. People sometimes ask about the differences between Haggadahs from faraway times and places. The differences can be interesting, but the consistency is important.

This continuity, vertical through the generations and horizontal across the continents, becomes possible when we realize just what the retelling and the reliving are facilitating: a conversation. We are asking the same questions, dreaming the same dreams, struggling with the same texts, and telling the same story as Jews have done around the world and across the ages. This is, literally, an eternal and omnipresent conversation—perhaps the greatest of all time.

What is this conversation about? The story of the Exodus, yes—defined broadly. It is, however, much more than that. The topics covered in the Haggadah include education; history; dreams; happiness; memory; parenthood; order; blessings; food; existential need; hunger; Jewish peoplehood; when to delegate; curiosity; music; beginnings; endings; the meanings of why, wisdom, and foolishness; when bad things happen to good people—and so much more.

1. Which of my guests from Seders past do I wish could be with me this year? What, imagining them here, would make them nourished by the experience and proud of me?

2. What are three topics that I want to be sure to have rigorous conversation about at the Seder?

The number and composition of subjects aroused in the Haggadah demonstrate just how pervasive, complicated, ambitious, and interesting the Jewish questions around freedom are.

—*THE TELLING,* P. 17

GOD'S BUSINESS CARD

Many of us have business cards. In life, our business cards contain a one-line description of who we are. And when we pass away, there will be one line on our gravestone. A clergyperson and/or loved one will give a eulogy that will attempt to encapsulate a life in a short speech.

But every one of us is more complex than what we can usually say about ourselves, or others can say about us. This fact is reflected in the Hebrew word *panim*. It means "face"—except that it is a plural word: It actually means "faces." There is no singular word for face in Hebrew, because no one has just one.

We exist in faces, but communicate in face.

In this (and everything else), we are created in God's image. What does it say on God's business card? One might expect something like "Creator of the Heavens and the Earth." These creations are, of course, his most impressive technical achievements, impossible for anyone to fully understand—let alone approximate.

Yet that is not what God chose. His is in the Ten Commandments: "I am Hashem Your God, who brought you out of the land of Egypt, out of slavery."

As explained in *The Telling* (p. 20), God chose to define himself not as the Creator but as the Liberator. Through this choice, God continues to tell us who he is—he who takes us from bad places and brings us to better places; he who takes us out of slavery and brings us to freedom.

God chose to define himself, in other words, by his mission and his purpose. As we are created in God's image, the message from the Torah and the Haggadah is clear and inspiring: We must have a mission and a purpose as well, worthy of our self-definition and complete commitment.

Some might wonder: God, being God, could easily figure out his mission and purpose. But how am I supposed to figure out mine?

The answer is that one's mission and purpose is always easy to figure out. In order to find it, each of us must ask of ourselves: What am I good (or even great) at? What do I enjoy doing? Toward what problems and opportunities do I gravitate?

1. What are you very good (or even great) at?

_____

_____

_____

_____

2. How might your unique talents help you to understand your mission and purpose?

_____

_____

_____

_____

3. What is your mission and purpose?

_____

_____

_____

_____

4. What are two steps you will take this year to achieve your mission and purpose?

_____

_____

_____

_____

> What should we put on our business card, and how should we act accordingly? For that, we have the Haggadah.
>
> —*THE TELLING*, P. 25

THE CRAZIEST DREAM COMES TRUE: HOW WE LIVE IN MOSES'S WORLD

Imagine if a politician, from any party, ran for office and *did not* say something like: "Our children are our future," or "Education is the most important issue for me," or "Education is the best investment we can make."

The inconceivability of such a possibility is not because emphasis on education is natural or normal. It is because of a choice that Moses made thousands of years ago. Moses had a challenge. He wanted, per Exodus 12:14, the Pesach Seder (and the Judaism it embodied) to last "as an eternal decree."

That's a long time, and a commensurately bold vision. How would Moses accomplish it? He placed his bet on the children. In Exodus 12:26, Moses said, "When your children ask you . . ." *When* your children ask? How did Moses know that any child, let alone all the children, would ask—and long into the future?

Because he had identified the fundamental characteristic of childhood. It is the characteristic expressed by the one word that every three-year-old says around twenty times an hour. And every parent and older sibling knows exactly what that word is!

How would curiosity perpetuate the Jewish people? Through, as Moses decreed, education. He lived in a world where the alphabet had barely been invented and where education was more likely to be criminalized than encouraged for thousands of years to follow. The reluctance of leaders to allow their people to be educated is quite sensible: Education leads to questions, and questions can lead to challenges to authority. Moses, the greatest psychologist of all, knew this, and he wasn't frightened by it. Rather, he counted on it. Education would not destabilize the Jewish people; it would enable, strengthen, and perpetuate us. Jewish memory and the future of the Jewish people would rely on mass education and universal literacy.

1. Judaism brought the idea of universal literacy and mass education to the world, and sustained it during the centuries when everyone else was either opposed or indifferent to it. We are the heirs to, and beneficiaries of, this great gift. How do you commit to improving your and/or your child's education in the coming year?

2. How will you make sure that education for your children continues throughout the summer months that are just around the corner?

3. One of the wonderful things about education and learning is that it (like candlelight, unlike material goods) increases to the extent that it is shared. How will you commit to improving the education of people outside your family and even your community?

> The idea that children should come first was a radical innovation that became a standard feature of Jewish life and then global culture.
>
> —*THE TELLING*, P. 29

GETTING READY: WHEN THE PREPARATION IS PART OF THE EVENT

Rabbi Joseph B. Soloveitchik said that everything holy involves preparation. This is best exemplified with the Pesach Seder, for which there are weeks of preparation—intellectual, spiritual, and practical. How should we prepare for Pesach?

The answer is revealed in what the Torah tells us about Pesach. Pesach, which per Exodus 12:2 occurs at the "head of months," is the Jewish New Year. Occurring, per Deuteronomy 16:1, "in the month of spring," it is also our spring festival.

Why, as discussed in *The Telling* (p. 9), do so many cultures have a spring festival? Because it is the season when we literally go outside again, and when the spirit of newness, renewal, and rejuvenation is in the air. This is the best time for a New Year, which presents us with the opportunity to take a spiritual inventory of ourselves now, to consider who we want to be in the coming year, and to make resolutions and commitments toward that end.

One might ask: Isn't Rosh Hashanah the New Year? Well, Rosh Hashanah is not in the Torah. It was the Babylonian New Year that we kept when we returned to Israel from Babylonia in 538 B.C.E. There are other New Years in Judaism as well. For example, the New Year of the trees is on the fifteenth day of Shevat—in mid-January.

This practice of having multiple New Years is echoed in American life. We have our calendar New Year on January 1, our national New Year on July 4, our personal New Year on our birthday, our relationship New Year on our anniversary, and our education New Year in September.

The reason for all of these New Years? The opportunity provided by a New Year, to understand who we are and who we can be, is too great to celebrate only once every twelve months.

But what *this* New Year is about is community and peoplehood. It is thus a New Year for relationships, with ourselves and with others, and that's what we should prepare to enrich.

1. Think about who will be at your Seder this year. How can you strengthen the relationships with three of those people? How can you strengthen your relationships with people who won't be there but should be?

2. How will you improve the preparation for the tasks that are important to you?

> Preparing for a pleasure and looking forward to it . . .
> doubles the feeling of enjoyment.
>
> —JUDAH HALEVI

SINGING THE TABLE OF CONTENTS: WHY HIGHLY RELIGIOUS MARRIED WOMEN ARE SO SEXUALLY SATISFIED

In addition to being the Jewish New Year, Pesach is the Festival of Freedom. It is rather strange—and thus, interesting—that we celebrate our Festival of Freedom with a ritual called Order (or Seder). This emphasis on order goes well beyond the name. We are so committed to the order that we begin the Seder by singing the table of contents.

In emphasizing the importance of order, we are teaching our children and reminding ourselves that freedom and order do not exist in opposition. Rather, they support and indeed need each other. Why does freedom need order? Freedom, if understood as the license to do whatever one wants as long as it does not harm anyone else, does not require order. But that is not freedom, at least in the biblical imagination. Every time Moses, channeling God, told Pharaoh, "Let my people go," he followed it with a variant of "so that they might serve." Freedom is the ability to act according to one's purpose. Freedom, therefore, is something to be done well. For that, it needs order.

This concept exists throughout Judaism. In addition to celebrating Pesach through the Seder (meaning "order"), our word for prayerbook, the book intended to help us develop the inspiration to grow spiritually, is *siddur* (also "order"). The Talmud, in Sotah 49a, asks: Why, in the midst of suffering, does the world continue to exist? The answer: *akdusha d'sidra* (literally "sanctification of the order").

The indispensability of order to doing freedom well is intuitive to anyone who has mastered anything. For instance, do I have the freedom right now to play beautiful music on the piano? On the one hand, sure—I can walk from where I'm sitting, completely unencumbered, to the piano and start playing. However, I don't even know what a chord is. In other words, I have not mastered the order of music. Consequently, I have the freedom to bang on the keys— but not to do anything beautiful, constructive, or worthy with it.

1. How do you want to live your freedom in the coming year?

2. How will you improve your mastery of order to optimize the practice of freedom—
   particularly around the area(s) discussed in your answer to the first question?

A table of contents is, of course, the order of a book. Most readers glance at the table of contents of a book and then move on quickly. This is not what happens with the Haggadah at the Seder. We sing it—yes, we sing the table of contents. On this Festival of Freedom, we are so insistent on order that we sing the table of contents. It is almost weird.

—*THE TELLING*, P. 53

MUSIC AND FOOD: THE THEOLOGY AND SCIENCE OF REMEMBERING

Let's stop for a moment and think about Pesachs past. What images and memories come to mind? We recall the people we were with, the places where we were, and perhaps even the ideas and insights that we and others shared. And we also remember two other things: the songs that we sang and the food that we ate.

The music and food of Pesach are so familiar that we might not stop to consider how interesting it is that they play such a large role in the Seder. Pesach is our great Jewish New Year celebration, when we are charged with taking an existential inventory of who we are now and who we want to be in the coming year—and making resolutions and commitments to bring us there. There is so much to accomplish on this most important of nights that the notion of "completing" the work is impossible to fathom.

Why, then, do we devote so much time to singing and all things related to food, including singing about it? Ought we not focus on learning from the Haggadah on Pesach night—and focus on music and food on any of the other nights of the year?

Modern brain science, as explained in *The Telling* (p. 57), offers an explanation. Our brains are primed to associate memories with music and food. Any evening, holiday, or event devoted to remembering would have to emphasize music and food.

1. What are your Pesach memories that relate to music and food?

_____

_____

_____

_____

2. What other powerful memories do you have that relate to music and food?

_____

_____

_____

_____

3. How might you use the magical properties of music and food to help instill memories that you want to carry long into your future and that of your family?

_____

_____

_____

_____

_____

> Those who wrote the Haggadah would not have known what is meant by a "reminiscence bump" or "evolutionary neuroscience," but they somehow knew that sustaining a memory would be best carried by matzah and maror (bitter herbs), dipping and dessert, and lots of singing.
>
> —*THE TELLING*, P. 59

WHAT WE CAN LEARN FROM AN EGG: THE LOGIC OF THE SEDER PLATE

There are many interpretations of the symbolism of the ritual objects on the Seder plate. Does the egg, the Jewish symbol of mourning, represent the cycle of life—showing that even in this time of joy we should acknowledge sorrow? Or does it represent the Jew—the more it is boiled, the tougher it gets?

Does the pasty charoset represent the bricks that we made while slaves in Egypt—reminding us of the oppression of our slavery? Or does it represent the apple trees under which we made love while slaves in Egypt—reminding us of the persistence of Jewish hope?

Yes to all.

1. What are the important symbols in your life?

2. What are the multiple meanings that each symbol has?

3. *The Telling* (pp. 60–61) lists several items on the Seder plate and their multiple meanings. Which of these meanings, or others, speaks the most to you?

> Understanding something as having multiple meanings is one of the deepest expressions of freedom.
>
> —RABBI ELIE KAUNFER

INVITE *THAT* SELF

Whoever is hungry—let him come and eat! Whoever is needy—let him come and celebrate Pesach!

This sounds like an invitation. But if it is an invitation, why are we issuing it when the Seder has already begun?

The answer is revealed in the Hebrew word *panim*. *Panim*, as noted earlier, means "faces"—and it is, crucially, in the plural. There is no Hebrew word for a singular face. And when a language does not have a word for something, it is because its culture does not have a concept of it. There is no Hebrew word for a singular "face" because no one has just one. We all have multiple faces—for instance, one that we wear in a job interview, one when playing with our child, one when relaxing with our spouse, one when praying in synagogue, and so many more.

Yet just one face is being invited to the Seder—that is, the face that is hungry and needy. In other words, the face being invited is the one that Jewish teaching emphasizes is especially beloved by God: our broken face.

As *The Telling* explains (p. 63), we are inviting our broken selves. At the conclusion of a good meal, we might say that we feel "satisfied." And the late president of Israel Shimon Peres said that the greatest Jewish contribution to humanity is "dissatisfaction." In other words, the "face" being invited to the Seder is our face that is dissatisfied. It is still hungry.

Why, then, needy? The most overrated goal in American life might be the achievement of "independence." Many people aspire to it for themselves and wish it for their children—but what is it? Independence is the state, literally, without need—when one doesn't need anybody and nobody needs him.

Judaism, as do all mature systems, rejects this. Instead, we seek interdependence. We look around the Seder table and see lots of people who need us, and lots of people whom we need.

1. What are you hungry for? What are you dissatisfied by? Let's name one thing that you are hungry to change about yourself. And let's name one thing you are hungry to change in the world.

2. How are you going to alleviate those hungers in the coming year?

3. Who, and what, do you *need*? Who needs you? How will you enlarge the circle of need in the coming year?

> There is nothing so whole as a broken heart.
>
> —THE KOTZKER REBBE

THE GREATEST PRINCIPLE OF THE TORAH

Whoever is hungry—let him come and eat! Whoever is needy—let him come and celebrate Pesach!

As discussed in *The Telling* (p. 72), Rabbi Akiva said that the "greatest principle of the Torah" is to "love the stranger." The originality and indeed radicalism of this idea that we should love the stranger is demonstrated by the fact that it is mentioned thirty-six times. The Torah never tells us to love our children, and doctors never tell us to be sure to go to the bathroom tomorrow. Why? For the same reason: We will do both uninstructed. However, we are told to love the stranger so many times because it is so unnatural and so important. This is in accordance with a learning from *The Telling*—that much of civilization, and perhaps of the moral life itself, is about overcoming what is natural in favor of what is right.

But what does it mean to "love the stranger"? Love, as Rabbi David Wolpe says, is an "enacted emotion"—it only exists in action. We know this in our relationships. If you told your spouse, "I love you," but never did anything to exemplify it, she would quickly and rightly conclude that your words were insincere and the relationship would suffer. The same is true with loving the stranger.

1. What "natural" instincts, temptations, or possibilities will you forsake this year in favor of what is good and right?

2. How will you fulfill your obligation to "love the stranger" in this coming year through practical action?

Anyone who becomes merciful upon the cruel will end up being cruel to the merciful.

—RABBI ELAZAR

JUST WHO ARE YOU CALLING A STRANGER?

Whoever is hungry—let him come and eat! Whoever is needy—let him come and celebrate Pesach!

We were slaves in Egypt—which the Torah and the historical record both show to be a completely brutal and horrific experience. Why, then, do we say that we were "strangers" rather than "slaves" in Egypt?

As *The Telling* shows (pp. 78–79), the Torah—and the Jewish teaching that follows—emphasizes that interpretation is a choice. There are usually multiple ways to interpret an experience or a circumstance, and we can choose the one that is best equipped to help us to have a happier, healthier, more hopeful, and better future.

1. What are two realities in your world (personal or communal) that you can interpret in very different ways? For instance, did something occur in your recent or distant past that plays a large role in your personal story?

2. How will you choose to interpret them productively?

> By teaching us to choose our interpretations, God is not only steering us from victimhood and the helplessness and hopelessness that it produces. He is offering a profound lesson in freedom.
>
> —*THE TELLING, P. 79*

LOVE AND RESPONSIBILITY: ISRAEL

Now, we are here; next year may we be in the Land of Israel!

For reasons explained in *The Telling* (p. 80), Judaism makes sense *only* with a strong, secure, vibrant, dynamic, and prosperous Israel. When we make the declaration at the Seder "Next year may we be in the Land of Israel," we are obligating ourselves to be in the Land of Israel in the coming year. We are not obligating ourselves to live there—but *to be* there, to have a meaningful presence in Israel. We can fulfill this by traveling to Israel, by advocating for Israel, by strengthening worthy institutions in Israel, by investing in Israel, and in many other ways.

1. How do you plan *to be* in the Land of Israel next year?

_____

_____

_____

_____

_____

_____

_____

_____

_____

_____

_____

_____

_____

_____

_____

_____

> What kind of people uses terms of romantic endearment (heart-Jerusalem) to describe a city? What kind of people, in its holy text, compares a city to a right hand and a tongue— and leaves the impression that the fullness of feeling is still incompletely expressed? What kind of people has sustained this love, in all its intensity, through thousands of years, hundreds of places, and the best and worst experiences that a people can have? A people in love.
>
> —*THE TELLING*, P. 83

JUDAISM IN A WORD: *NEWNESS*

Now we are slaves; next year may we be free men!

As we sit at beautiful Seders in Tel Aviv and Manhattan, in Miami and Toronto—we should ask: Did I just say that I was a slave?

Yes. And the first reaction to this should be discordance. As we recognize and appreciate our freedom, we should also note a hideous fact: There are more people living in slavery today than at any time in human history. This includes chattel slaves in Mauritania, fishing slaves on Lake Volta in Ghana, construction slaves in North Korea, road-building slaves in Laos, cotton-picking slaves in Uzbekistan, domestic slaves in China, mining slaves in the Democratic Republic of the Congo, tea and rice farming slaves in South Asia, the slaves who built the stadiums for the 2022 World Cup in Qatar, child soldier slaves in Iran, and sex slaves throughout the world.

There are slaves within ten miles of every Seder being held in an American city.

Yet we also said that *we* are slaves. How might we be slaves? We are certainly not slaves in any juridical sense. Having acknowledged that, we can explore a metaphorical possibility. What does every slave have in common? No slave has any control over her time.

What is the opposite of having no control over one's time? How, by extension, can we best be free?

The opposite of having no control over one's time is to sanctify time. How might we sanctify time?

First, imagine standing in a long line at the supermarket. You are frustrated. What are your options? You could curse yourself for coming at this hour, rather than a little later when the lines will surely be shorter. You could curse the guy in front of you for being so slow in unloading his cart. You could curse the supermarket management for not opening the aisle to the right.

Alternatively, you could take out your phone and call your great-aunt who is lonely and with whom you haven't spoken in too long. You could study Torah. You could identify a teacher from high school and message her about how much she meant to you. You could make a charitable donation on your phone.

Second, *The Telling* shows (p. 90) how to live longer—and why it works. This is by experiencing new things. Live your freedom by learning and experiencing something new.

1. What will you do, personally, this year, to help eliminate the evil of slavery—and to help actual slaves become free people?

2. How will you sanctify time in two ways in the coming two weeks?

> We should pursue new experiences and form new relationships; we should find what is special and distinctive in familiar things; we should allow ourselves to "begin again." It is by experiencing newness that we make life both longer and better.
>
> —*THE TELLING, P. 92*

THERE IS SUCH A THING AS A BAD QUESTION—AND SOMETIMES A GOOD REASON FOR IT

Why is this night different from all other nights?

The Four Questions have been a staple at everyone's Seder. Their intention is to arouse the interest of the children. Yet, has any child ever leapt from her chair and said: "Oh my God, we're dipping twice! Tell me the story of the Exodus!"

No. Therefore, why haven't these four questions been replaced with better ones at any point in the last two thousand years?

It is to show us that generic education is, at most, mediocre. We know what works. It is when a teacher (who could be a parent, a friend, or a professional educator) taps into what is unique about the student. This happens when the teacher tells the young student that her questions and disposition are those of a future great doctor, when the teacher remarks that the student's ability to combine a love of baseball with statistical understanding can lead to a great sports career, when the teacher tells the student that her essay on the biblical Joseph made her think of this book that she loved long ago. Genuine education, which inspires students and leads them to their calling, is always done with regard to the sacred uniqueness within each pupil.

1. Maimonides suggested that Seder leaders give children "roasted seeds and nuts" and take away the table before the Seder. Rabbi Chaim Soloveitchik would come to the Seder wearing a pot on his head. How will you arouse the interest of the specific children at your Seder?

2. How, recognizing that generic education does not work and that all children are unique, will you educate your children (and perhaps others) differently and creatively in the coming year?

> The Haggadah might be the ultimate guidebook, but there always remains a distinction between guidance and instruction.
>
> —*THE TELLING, P. 97*

THE GREAT JEWISH PERMISSION

We were slaves to Pharaoh in Egypt.
Our ancestors were idol worshippers.

There are two, and possibly four, beginnings in the Haggadah. Any Jewish story—and any telling or retelling of a Jewish story—would need multiple beginnings. Elie Wiesel said, "When he created man, God gave him a secret—and that secret was not how to begin, but how to begin again."

This "beginning again" has enabled several moral inventions that make our world possible. One is forgiveness, an idea conceived in the Torah. What question does forgiveness ask? It asks: Can we begin our relationship again, better?

1. What do you want to begin again in the coming year?

_____

_____

_____

_____

_____

_____

_____

_____

2. Who should you forgive? From whom do you want forgiveness? How will you earn it?

_____

_____

_____

_____

_____

_____

_____

_____

_____

Very few things in Judaism happen in private, and beginning again—though it requires soulful introspection and existential moral yearning—is not one of them.

—*THE TELLING*, P. 102

THE GREATEST SEDER OF ALL

Had the Holy One, Blessed is he, not taken our fathers out of Egypt, then we, our children, and our children's children would have remained subservient to Pharaoh in Egypt.

The Pesach Seder is an act of retelling and reliving the Exodus from Egypt. What, then, is the greatest Seder ever conducted? American history. From John Winthrop to Benjamin Franklin, from Harriet Tubman to Martin Luther King Jr., from the slaves yearning for freedom to the Architect of the Capitol, from George W. Bush to Barack Obama, those who dreamed American and acted accordingly were directly inspired by the Exodus story. They made the United States a living freedom story.

1. What is the most meaningful moment, to you, in American history that was directly inspired by the Exodus story?

_____

_____

_____

_____

2. How will you make your life a Seder?

_____

_____

_____

_____

_____

3. What are the three lessons of the Exodus that most compel you to action in the coming year?

_____

_____

_____

_____

_____

> The Hebraic Christian tradition is clear, however, in affirming that in the long struggle between good and evil, good eventually emerges as the victor.
>
> —MARTIN LUTHER KING JR.

FEELING GOD'S PLEASURE

Even if we were all men of wisdom, understanding, experience, and knowledge of the Torah—
it would still be an obligation upon us to tell about the Exodus from Egypt.

Has anyone ever claimed that they do not need to participate in a Seder because they are "wise, understanding, experienced, and knowledgeable"? Presumably not.

So why is this passage here?

As the eleventh-century rabbi Abraham ben Meir Ibn Ezra said, "The core of all the commandments is the improvement of character—and the majority of them are essentially reminders." This is the case with the festivals of Pesach and Sukkot, hearing the shofar, affixing mezuzot, and wearing tzitzit—and many others. We all need reminders to keep us on our spiritual track.

The Telling (p. 116) brings other examples of how reminding is crucially used both in modern Jewish practice and secular living.

1. What are two important practices in your life that you would perform better given a system of reminders?

_____

_____

_____

_____

_____

_____

_____

_____

2. How will you implement, in the most practical way, these reminders?

_____

_____

_____

_____

_____

_____

_____

_____

> If we put a memento of our beloved grandmother on our desk, will we be likelier to be honest in business? If we see a photograph of our toddler by the dashboard, will we be likelier to drive more safely?
>
> —*THE TELLING*, P. 116

THE STORY IS YOURS: WHERE ARE MOSES, JOSEPH, AND THE WOMEN OF THE EXODUS?

The more one tells about the discussion of the Exodus, the more he is praiseworthy.

Imagine: A teacher gives a student an assignment to tell the story of the Exodus. The student returns with an essay that does not mention Moses, Joseph, Miriam, Puah, Shifra, or the Pharaoh's daughter.

The teacher would have, effectively, two choices. She could give the child an F. Or she could conclude that the child was operating by an entirely different logic and contemplate awarding an A+.

The student's work could be the Haggadah.

Why would the Haggadah not mention any of these indispensable characters from the Exodus story?

To teach us an important lesson: When it comes to the most important things in our lives, such as the education of our children, there can be no outsourcing. Our children's school may be fantastic, but even the best is only part of the education process. The Haggadah may be the greatest guidebook ever written, but that's all it is—a guidebook. It cannot do our job for us. We have to teach the story to our children, incorporating Moses, Joseph, and the women of the Exodus. And we should do so in a way that we think will work best for our children, fulfilling our biblically ordained roles as parents/educators.

1. What are the tasks in your life that you can never outsource, and will always require your significant involvement?

_____

_____

_____

_____

_____

_____

_____

_____

_____

2. How do you want to change your practices regarding what you do yourself and what others do for you?

_____

_____

_____

_____

_____

_____

_____

_____

_____

> The Haggadah requires us to tell the story by reaching outside the Haggadah!
>
> —*THE TELLING*, P. 120

LIVING BY PRINCIPLES

It happened that Rabbi Eliezer, Rabbi Joshua, Rabbi Elazar ben Azariah, Rabbi Akiva, and Rabbi Tarfon . . .

These are five of the greatest rabbis of all time. This Seder is for Judaism what the 1992 United States men's Olympic basketball team is for sport and the American Constitutional Convention is for political thought. There will never be such a collection of talent in one place at one time, doing their craft together.

The Haggadah tells us that their Seder lasted until the morning hours, when their students entered and told them that it was time for the morning Shema. There are thousands of people who have names in the Torah, showing that Jewish teaching tries to make as many people as possible feel distinctive, important, and valued—which is what calling someone by their name demonstrates.

Yet these students—none of whom is named—had the confidence to instruct their great teachers that it was time to conclude the Seder and fulfill their current obligation (to say the morning prayers). And these students also had the authority to do so, as their act is immortalized in the Haggadah and celebrated by Seder-goers around the world and throughout history.

Why did the students feel so confident?

The most prevalent command in the Torah is "do not fear." And they did not.

1. When have you felt the need to challenge, on the basis of shared principles, the position of someone in a superior role?

_____

_____

_____

_____

_____

_____

_____

_____

_____

_____

2. How might you do so in the coming year?

_____

_____

_____

_____

_____

_____

_____

_____

How do the teachers respond? The Haggadah does not tell us because it does not need to. Their delight leaps off the page.

—*THE TELLING*, P. 124

HUMILITY CAN BE A SIN

Rabbi Elazar ben Azariah said, "I am like a seventy-year-old man . . ."

When Rabbi Elazar ben Azariah said that he had the wisdom of a seventy-year-old man, he was approximately sixteen years old. We normally counsel bragging adolescents to exit that phase of their lives quickly, en route to a more mature stage. Why, then, are we immortalizing the bragging of an adolescent in our sacred text?

This passage teaches us the true meaning of humility. It is perfectly articulated by the truth often associated with the Christian writer C. S. Lewis, who said: "Humility is not thinking less of yourself. It is thinking of yourself less."

There are many examples of our greatest people—Jacob, Joseph, Moses—being fully aware of their extraordinary gifts and talents, being very comfortable acknowledging them. Humility, we see through these examples, consists of acknowledging one's God-given gifts while directing them in the service of a God-given mission. By contrast, Jewish teaching considers false humility—the refusal to acknowledge our great God-given gifts—to be a sin. And God models this. In the Torah, he acknowledges his early work as "good" or "very good"—and later frequently refers to his strength and righteousness.

As with God, so with his partner—humanity. It is only after fully acknowledging our divinely provided gifts, by recognizing what mighty staff God has put in our hand, by appreciating the uniqueness of our great talent and capability, that we can do God's will on earth. This is what it means to create a dwelling place for God on earth.

The Rebbe Menachem Mendel Schneerson considered the Talmudic expression that every Jew is a guarantor for every other Jew. This expression, he said, is only meaningful in the context of acknowledging that every Jew must be richer, in some way, than every other Jew. After all—as everyone who has had a loan or a rental guaranteed knows—a guarantee only makes sense if the guarantor is richer than the person whose obligation he is guaranteeing. Consequently, every Jew must be richer than every other Jew in some way.

Of course, the Rebbe's logic does not apply only to Jews. It applies to every community. In fact, the definition of a community might be a group of people who agree to be each other's guarantors. Consequently, each member of the community must be richer than every other member in some way. In order for the community to function optimally, each member must identify his or her oversized talent—and contribute it to the betterment of the community.

1. What great gift or talent has God given to you?

_____

_____

_____

_____

2. How will you use that gift to improve the world, and to make God proud?

_____

_____

_____

_____

3. What can all the talented and gifted people at your Seder accomplish together?

_____

_____

_____

_____

_____

_____

> Life is not a gift; it's a loan.
>
> —RABBI MOSHE SCHEINER

WHEN TO FIND GOD

The phrase "the days of your life" would have indicated only the days; the addition of the word "all" includes the nights as well.

When Rabbi Elazar ben Azariah finished bragging about his wisdom, what did he talk about? He said that the phrase "days of your life" encompasses the nights, too.

This seems odd. He had the attention of several of the greatest rabbis in Jewish history—and, for that matter, all Seder-goers for all time as well. And this is what he chose to discuss?

Yes. Because our prodigy was not only discussing a timing issue. He was discussing the nature of God. Jewish tradition emphasizes, for reasons articulated in *The Telling* (pp. 132–133), what God wants with us: a relationship. And what characterizes a genuine relationship? Consistency. A genuine relationship is one that flourishes in the darkness and in the light, the night and the day, of our lives.

1. Do you relate to God better in the day of your life (when things are going well) or in the night (during times of loss, disappointment, and suffering)?

2. How can you prepare, in the year ahead, to strengthen your relationship with God in the times of your life when you relate to God with less closeness?

> A relationship with God is not one for tactical use. He is not the doctor we call when we get sick or the event planner we call when we want to celebrate. He is not a nocturnal terror manager or an afternoon cheerleader. He is the pillar of cloud who cools the day and the pillar of fire who warms the night.
>
> —*THE TELLING*, P. 133

COMMITMENT

But the Sages declare that "the days of your life" would mean only the present world; the addition of "all" includes the era of the Messiah.

There is no mention of a Messiah in the Torah. But later teachings emphasize that the Messiah will change everything. Even pigs, that most unkosher of animals, will, according to some, become kosher when the Messiah comes! Why, then, would the authors of the Haggadah devote a section to emphasizing that the word *all* means something specific—that the Seder must be celebrated subsequent to the arrival of the Messiah?

To teach us about commitment. As events accumulate, the importance of previous events naturally recedes in our minds. How can we be sure that the same will not happen with an event that happened long ago—the Exodus from Egypt, for example—and whose importance we want always to sustain us? By making a commitment—even an appointment—to continue the celebration after the Messiah comes.

1. What events (personally or otherwise) do you want your children always to remember with intensity and purpose, regardless of how much time passes?

_____

_____

_____

_____

2. What very practical tactics, like the Haggadah and the Seder, will you use to sustain the memory of the events that you want to keep at the forefront of the minds of your children?

_____

_____

_____

_____

_____

3. For the children: What is your favorite memory that you'll remember from this year's Seder? (Make a note of it, and revisit five years from now.)

_____

_____

_____

_____

> The Messiah may reset everything in the world, but not our commitment to telling the story of the Exodus in the way that we do.
>
> —THE TELLING, P. 135

THE JEWISH SECRET OF PARENTING

Concerning four sons does the Torah speak—one wise one, one wicked one, one simple one, and one who is unable to ask.

Why are there four sons at the Seder? The answer is revealed in that each child is introduced as "one"—as in, "one wise son, one wicked son." The word *one* (*echad*) has an unmistakable association in the Bible. From Deuteronomy to Zacharia to Job, it refers to the oneness unique to God.

As we know from Genesis 1:27, each person is created in the image of God. This is recognized through our having multiple children. Why four? Because the night is too short for there to be 400,000. There could be a curious child and an enthusiastic child, a sullen child and a loquacious child—but four is the largest number of hypothetical children that could be practically accommodated.

The practical implications? We see that our God is a big God, with many legitimate ways to access him. If there are many ways to arrive at wherever each of us is right now, imagine how many more ways there must be to access our infinite God! Some children are mechanical and some are musical, some are intellectual and some are prayerful, some are physical and some are introspective—and each has a unique way to access God.

1. How might each of the children in your life uniquely access God?

2. How can you, as a parent/teacher/leader, help each child to use her unique strengths to access God?

3. Which of the "sons" do you think is most similar to you, at this moment?

> The Jewish way to create a sacred and enduring community with common values and a shared vision is by respecting the uniqueness of each participant. It is by enabling each member to identify and develop what he can uniquely contribute that the community becomes stronger.
>
> —*THE TELLING,* P. 138

HOW INTELLECTUAL INQUIRY IS OF LIMITED VALUE: CONSIDERING THE WISE SON

The great Catholic historian Paul Johnson said that Judaism is "an ancient and highly efficient social machine for the production of intellectuals." This is a fine and fair description of a tradition that deeply values learning and education. Indeed we often call ourselves "the people of the book" and we conduct our New Year's celebration—the Pesach Seder—guided by a book (the Haggadah) in a highly cerebral experience.

It is in that context that we can understand, and learn from, the response to the wise son. The wise son asks a question that is entirely intellectual. And the answer is about . . . dessert. And the fundamental quality of dessert? Taste.

All intellectual inquiry, the parent is instructing the wise child, must be done in accordance with the taste test. The wise child, and all of us who are intellectually inclined, should ask: "How will these ideas that I hold dear play out in the real world where real people are experiencing life in accordance with them?"

1. How might the ideas that you hold dear have unintended consequences of which you should be especially mindful?

2. Where else, even outside pure intellectual inquiry, might you apply the taste test? In certain behaviors, practices, and activities?

> How does one love God with his evil impulse? Judaism posits two ways: by channeling to create good or structuring to prevent bad.
>
> —*THE TELLING*, P. 139

THE FUNDAMENTAL PRINCIPLE OF JUDAISM: CONSIDERING THE WICKED SON

The first thing to consider about the wicked son is his age. This son cannot be a toddler, as toddlers are not wicked, and they do not ask text-based questions. Indeed, we all know this child—he is rolling his eyes rather than answering questions, texting in the middle of the Seder, distracting the other Seder-goers with his behavior, and generally demonstrating and projecting disrespect for the Seder and its attendees.

He is probably between fifteen and nineteen years old. Why is that important? Because while a toddler has to be where we put him and go where we send him, a teenager has freedom of movement. If a teenager does not want to be at the Seder, he won't be at the Seder. The wicked son has decided to come to the Seder. So, while we may, rightly, focus on how he is different from his siblings in the Haggadah, we should as well consider how he is different from the fifth child—the one who decided not to come to the Seder.

The wicked son, for whatever reason, is at the Seder. And that presence means that his parents, and the Jewish tradition they represent, have a lifeline to him.

Still, his question, as *The Telling* explains (pp. 149–150), is wicked.

In response to this question, the authors of the Haggadah suspend their role as storytellers and assume that of pundits. And their commentary is on all of Judaism—appropriate, as the Haggadah is the Greatest Hits of Jewish Thought, and Pesach is our glorious New Year. They opine that the fundamental principle of Judaism is membership in the community.

Then, in a short sequence (examined in *The Telling*, p. 152), the authors of the Haggadah tell us how to redeem a wicked son.

And the wicked son is just an example of the wayward child. The many and profound lessons in the short response to the wicked son serve all parents and teachers who have a child to redeem.

1. The Seder you are attending this year may be predominantly liberal, or it may be predominantly traditional. What are three characteristics of the Judaism practiced at the other kind of Seder that you find most compelling? How might you bring those characteristics into your conception or practice of Judaism?

2. In accordance with the parent of the wicked son, what are two ways that you can acknowledge to your wayward child how you (as a parent) may have contributed to the behavior that now disappoints you?

3. If your children are young, but not wayward, what are three commitments that you can make to ensure that they find their own true and inspired path—and not go wayward?

And what does the father learn? That a wicked son could not only become wise, but also righteous.

—*THE TELLING, P. 157*

WHO IS THE IDEAL HUSBAND? CONSIDERING THE SIMPLE SON

As explained in *The Telling* (p. 159), the simple son is many things—but he is not stupid. The term for "simple" (*tam*) is used often in the Torah, as in (per Deuteronomy 18:13): "Be *tamim* with the Lord your God."

This is not God saying, "Be stupid with me." It is God saying, "Be wholehearted with me."

The *tam* is not like his sibling, the wise child. He may be as smart as anyone. Jacob, who the Torah also calls a *tam,* was a genius in business, agriculture, and faith. The simple son just does not approach God as his wise brother does. The simple son's questions are not highly intellectual. His approach does not involve making complex textual distinctions and he does not wrestle with religious concepts to find his place in the world.

He is the neighbor whose Independence Day barbeque is the best party of the year, the member of the synagogue or church who volunteers his time whenever there is a need, the person who everyone knows is on call to help all the time.

He is wholehearted, always reliable, and completely dependable.

1. Who would you rather marry—or who would you rather your child or sibling marry: the wise son or the simple son?

_____

_____

_____

_____

_____

_____

_____

_____

_____

_____

_____

_____

_____

_____

_____

_____

_____

_____

_____

_____

> The wholehearted son in the Haggadah asks *only,*
> "What is this?" He is concerned only about the essence
> of the Pesach experience.
>
> —*THE TELLING,* P. 160

WHAT SHOULD WE BE ASKING? CONSIDERING THE SON WHO DOES NOT KNOW HOW TO ASK

Like the wicked son, this son is not a toddler. A toddler will grow out of that stage, and thus doesn't need a specific question—especially when there are an infinite number of possibilities and only time for four. Moreover, most parents know how to educate a child of that age at the Seder. We encourage them to smell the smells, eat the food, hear the music and, most importantly, feel the love (of the Jewish tradition and of each other) in the room.

One of the greatest rabbis in modern times was Rav Levi Yitzchak of Berditchev. He lived in what is now Poland in the eighteenth century. When he came to this part in the Seder, he would grow very pensive. Then he would say what was on his mind: that he was the son who did not know how to ask a question. He would then pray to God to reveal the right questions to him.

Looking back on the mistakes we've made in life, did we make those mistakes because we came up with the wrong answer to the right question—or because we didn't ask the right question in the first place? More often than not, we will conclude the latter. Once we have the right question, the answer is often easier to come by. It is conceiving of the right question that can be difficult, and it is our failure to do it that results in our mistakes. Consequently, we are each the fourth son. This son reminds each of us to pray that God give us the strength and wisdom to know what questions to ask.

1. What questions, in your personal life, should you ask as you enter the New Year?

_____

_____

_____

_____

_____

_____

_____

_____

2. What questions, in your professional life, should you ask as you enter the New Year?

_____

_____

_____

_____

_____

_____

_____

_____

> God of Abraham, Isaac, and Jacob, the fourth son, he who does not even know how to ask a question, that is me, Levi Yitzchak. If I only knew how to ask questions, I would ask you these questions. Read them into my heart, Almighty God.
>
> **—RAV LEVI YITZCHAK OF BERDITCHEV**

FINDING THE IMAGE OF GOD
(IT'S NOT HARD)

Originally, our ancestors were idol worshippers.

We begin the story of the Exodus by declaring our beginning as "idolaters." Most people(s) begin their stories in glory, often through divinity or near-divinity. We do so as idolaters. The severity of the prohibition on idolatry in Judaism cannot be overstated. It is the most prohibited activity in the Torah, and Maimonides, channeling the Talmud, says that the denial of idolatry is akin to accepting the whole Torah.

Moreover, the Haggadah does not even let us make this a story of human accomplishment. It allows that we are now "nearer to his service." In other words, we must still be struggling with idolatry. And since we are not still worshipping stone dogs, idolatry must be something much different and far more pervasive than we might imagine.

Idolatry is, for reasons explained in *The Telling* (pp. 163–165), the act of providing one's ultimate allegiance to anything or anybody other than God. Everything in the world can be a tool we can use to serve God—or it can be an idol that we serve itself. This applies to money, beauty, physical pleasure, recognition, and anything else.

Whether an item is a holy object or an idol is up to us.

1. What do you worship that isn't God?

_____

_____

_____

_____

_____

_____

_____

_____

_____

2. In the coming year, what four steps will you take to be "nearer to God"—and further from idolatry?

_____

_____

_____

_____

_____

_____

_____

_____

_____

_____

> It is precisely because God has an image that idols are forbidden. You are the image of God. Every human being is God's image.
>
> —ABRAHAM JOSHUA HESCHEL

IDENTIFY ENEMIES— AND ALSO FRIENDS

It is this that has stood by our fathers and us. For not only one has risen against us to annihilate us, but in every generation.

This is one of the moments in the Haggadah when we participate in both a vertical and a horizontal conversation. Pesach was, for many years, a time of terror. It was a time when the vicious rumors and lies of Jew haters were ripe, with unthinkable suffering to follow. *The Telling* provides many such examples from throughout history (pp. 166–167).

We live in a very different world today, but there are still Jews who would recognize the truth in this statement all too well. These are the Jews in Iran and the Jews in Israel within missile range of Iran, Hezbollah, and Hamas.

The tragic fact, as noted in the Haggadah, is that in every generation there are those who try to annihilate us.

However, as *The Telling* shows (p. 171), there has been an entirely new dynamic in the world. We still have enemies, as we always have had. We must identify them accurately. But now, we have a large, powerful, and growing number of friends. Many of these new friends are Evangelical Christians—tens and perhaps hundreds of millions of people who love all things Jewish: the Jewish religion, the Jewish state, Jewish teachings, and the Jewish people.

In the Book of Numbers, the gentile seer Balaam cursed the Jews when he said that we will be a people who "dwells alone."

Now, for the first time, we are not alone. The curse has, after thousands of years, been lifted.

1. How will you protect the Jews against the enemies in this generation?

_____

_____

_____

_____

_____

_____

2. How will you participate and build this new and great friendship between Jews and gentile peoples?

_____

_____

_____

_____

_____

_____

> Jews have never had anything like the friends we have in the twenty-first century, especially, but not exclusively, among Evangelical Christians . . . We may not know what it all means, but we are certainly in the early stages of living the dream of Deuteronomy 32:43: "The nations will sing praises for His people!"
>
> —*THE TELLING*, P. 172

THE JEWISH WAY OF LEARNING

Go and learn what Laban the Aramean attempted to do to our father Jacob!

"Go and learn" is a strange, and thus intriguing and instructive locution. When we instruct a pupil, we would normally say, "Come and learn." Yet, we say "go" to reflect the Jewish way of learning. Jewish learning is an eternal dialectic between book learning and experience. We take our book learning into the world, and our world into our book learning—acquiring knowledge through the combination. One without the other will not provide the education envisioned by the authors of the Haggadah. *The Telling* shows (p. 174) how this philosophy was operationalized by rabbis in ancient times and by the system that produced them.

By choosing "go" in reference to Laban (a complicated and malicious man) the authors of the Haggadah are demonstrating which form of learning they regard as more fundamental. Jewish learning requires "going," which is to say it requires action. We are to bring our worldly learnings to our understanding of Torah, and our understanding of Torah to our worldly engagements.

1. How do you acquire knowledge of how people act and why they do so—in the course of your "going"?

_____

_____

_____

_____

_____

_____

_____

2. How will you best learn—through books and experience, by studying and worldly involvement—in the coming year?

_____

_____

_____

_____

_____

_____

_____

Our greatest rabbis were goers. They had professions that they practiced regularly . . . Rabbi Jose was a tanner, Rav Huna was a water carrier, Rabbi Joshua was a blacksmith, Rabbi Akiva was a shepherd, and Hillel the Elder was a woodcutter.

—*THE TELLING*, P. 174

DESTINY'S INGREDIENTS: FAMILY AND DREAMS

For Pharaoh decreed only against the males, and Laban attempted to uproot everything.

Why is Laban, a selfish manipulator, considered by the Haggadah to be worse than Pharaoh—a brutal slave master who invented (among other things) eliminationist Jew hatred?

Laban, as explained in *The Telling* (pp. 176–179), dealt two lasting and potentially existential blows against the Jews. First, he violated the fundamental rule of parenthood in sowing jealousy and dissension between his daughters by engineering a situation so both of them would marry Jacob. His strike against the integrity of his family would reverberate through the generations, and lead to the Egyptian slavery.

Second, something very significant happened to Jacob during his two-decade stay with his father-in-law. Prior to entry, he had dreamed the great Jewish dream—of angels climbing up and down the ladder, of uniting heaven and earth. Near the end of his stay (when he decided that he had to leave), he dreamed of spotted and speckled sheep—of material gain devoid of any spiritual purpose.

The time spent in the land of Laban had changed Jacob's dream. By placing such significance on Laban—by suggesting that he is worse than Pharaoh—the authors of the Haggadah are teaching us the most important thing we do. It is to dream. You can only be the person you want to be, and do the things you want to do, after you dream of them. And the most important way that we can influence others is by helping them dream.

1. What do you dream for yourself in the coming year?

_____

_____

_____

_____

_____

_____

_____

_____

2. What specific dreams do you have for at least one other person at your Seder in the coming year?

_____

_____

_____

_____

_____

_____

_____

_____

Whoever governs one's dreams—whether a parent, a sacred text, a leader, a peer, or someone or something else—largely determines who that person will become.

—*THE TELLING*, P. 179

IMAGINATION: THE MOST IMPORTANT PART OF REALITY

An Aramean attempted to destroy my father. Then he descended to Egypt, and sojourned there.

This is the part of the Haggadah when we finally get around to telling the story of the Exodus from Egypt. But we don't do so with Moses, or even with the text of Exodus. We do so with a farmer—an imaginary man in a time far in the future in the Land of Israel that no one in the Exodus story had seen.

Why do we tell the story so indirectly—not by way of any of its many participants, but through the lens of an imaginary man far in the future?

To teach us the importance of the imagination. Imagination is fundamental to our lives. It informs what we order for dinner, as we imagine which dish we will enjoy most. It informs what subjects we will emphasize at the Seder, as we imagine what will resonate with the attendees. It informs who we will marry, as we imagine whether we will be happier with this person or another.

1. What important decisions in your life have been a function of your imagination?

2. What important decisions do you face right now that involve your imagination?

3. How might a thoughtful, rigorous, and considered approach to the imagination help you to make a better decision?

4. One of the several problems with idolatry is that it represents the theology of the quick fix. We sometimes yearn for quick fixes (do something for the idol, and everything will be okay), but they never work and usually exacerbate the problem. Where in your life might you be turning to quick fixes instead of the honest encounter and hard work that is really needed for solutions?

> The imagination enables us to determine what possibilities might exist, where we want to go, who we want to be, what we want to know, what we should do, what we can expect of others and of ourselves.
>
> —*THE TELLING*, P. 183

JUDAISM: A RELIGION OF CHARACTER

Is Judaism a religion of action or character? Yes. It is, as explained in *The Telling* (pp. 184–189), a religion of both.

It is most apparent that Judaism is a religion of action—as the Torah expects us to *do* so much, from honoring our parents to eating only permitted foods to loving the stranger and so much more. And many of these requirements and expectations of action come through in the Haggadah, as they would in every serious Jewish expression.

When the Haggadah finally starts to tell the story of the Exodus, it does so through a farmer from the future—a man of Moses's imagination. The striking characteristic of the farmer, which comes through very clearly in the Deuteronomy text, is that he is awash in gratitude. By having us tell the story of our past in this way, the authors of the Haggadah are telling us how to feel and be on Pesach night and whenever we consider the Exodus (which should be every day): We should feel and be in a state of gratitude. The first action that observant Jews do upon waking from sleep is to say the *Modeh Ani* prayer that begins with "Grateful am I." We acknowledge the existence of gratitude before we acknowledge the existence of the self—and enable gratitude to define our approach to the coming day.

The subtle and striking instruction that it matters how we feel and who we are when we do something is a consistent Jewish theme. The *kohen gadol* (High Priest) is only allowed to bless the people if he can do so "with love."

Why, so long as the work gets done and the actions get taken, does it matter how we feel during their performance? *The Telling* goes through several key reasons, explaining how righteous action and good character are fundamentally inseparable (p. 186).

1. What are ten things you are grateful for? Be as specific as possible, and give reasons for your gratitude in each example. For instance, you might say that you are grateful for your daughter—but don't stop there. List several things about her that constitute and amplify that gratitude. This exercise will deepen your appreciation for the things you are grateful for, lead to your discovery of more sources of gratitude—and better help you to approach each day in gratitude.

2. What character trait do you want to cultivate in the coming year? What actions (additional or entirely new) will you take to develop that trait?

> A good society depends on people doing the right thing not because they have to but because they want to. And one of the functions of the rules and lessons from the Torah is to teach people how to act and think in their absence.
>
> —*THE TELLING*, P. 190

YOU ARE IN THE STORY

With seventy persons, your forefathers descended to Egypt.

Seven is, for reasons discussed in *The Telling* (p. 192), Judaism's holiest number. So, it would be reasonable that the start of the Jewish nation—the people who descended to Egypt—would consist of seventy people.

But there is a problem. The Torah, in Genesis 46, lists only sixty-nine of Jacob's household who came down to Egypt.

Why, then, would the Torah and the Haggadah tell us that seventy people descended to Egypt? Is this a basic error of arithmetic that has not been corrected in thousands of years? Or is the text trying to teach us something?

Indeed, the very nature of Pesach enables us to learn the intended lesson. The beginning of the Haggadah declares, "In every generation, we are obligated to see ourselves as though we personally came out of Egypt."

As discussed in *The Telling,* there is no ancient Hebrew word for "history." And when a language does not have a word for something, its culture does not have a concept of that thing. We have no concept of history—the chronicle of what happens to others. What we have is a very rich concept of memory—the chronicle of what is happening to us. The Jewish experience has no Jewish "them." It does not have a group of people who lived long ago and/or far away, and whose experience is fundamentally disconnected from ours. The Jewish story is a long, consistent, and coherent one. We are not its students, its observers, or its commentators. We are its participants.

Each of us is number seventy.

1. How can you relate to the Jewish experience more as memory than as history?

_____

_____

_____

_____

_____

2. How will you be a better #70 this year?

_____

_____

_____

_____

_____

3. When did you show up to a challenge? Why did it matter?

_____

_____

_____

_____

> The perpetuation of the story and the continuation of the Jewish people depend on each one of us. We are neither historians nor observers, we are neither commentators nor celebrants. We are participants.
>
> —*THE TELLING,* P. 193

STARS

Now Hashem, your God, has made you as numerous as the stars of Heaven.

Why would the Haggadah, following the Torah in many places, compare Jews to stars? If one were charged with describing the Jews today, the answer would likely not be: "The Jews! There are a lot of them."

The Telling explores several of the reasons why Jews are compared to stars. First, we are numerous by the measure of what anyone in biblical times would have reasonably predicted.

But perhaps more to the point, every star is unique. Thus, we learn that each of us is unique and special to God—and should be to each other as well.

There are several countings in the Torah in the context of censuses. In each case, it is forbidden to count the people. Instead, their contributions (in the form of a half shekel) are counted—the same contribution each with its unique character.

Alternatively, the way to navigate at night in ancient times was by the stars. This is what it means to be the chosen people—we are to be what the prophet Isaiah called "a light unto the nations." We should aspire to be the people that other peoples want to follow.

1. How will you, through your contributions, become a unique star in the year ahead?

_____
_____
_____
_____
_____
_____
_____
_____
_____
_____
_____
_____
_____
_____
_____
_____
_____

> The goodness of the community . . . is a function of the character of its individual inhabitants. And the character of its individual inhabitants, as we learn from the stars, will be determined to the extent that each person realizes that his sacred uniqueness is appreciated by God.
>
> —THE TELLING, P. 197

RISKING CONGRATULATIONS

Numerous—as it says: I made you as numerous as the plants of the field; you grew and developed, and became charming, beautiful of figure; your hair grown long; but you were naked and bare. And I passed over you and saw you downtrodden in your blood and I said to you: "Through your blood shall you live!"

This passage from Ezekiel 16, referred to as "two bloods" and what the Talmud calls "the chapter of rebuke," describes Jerusalem's descent into depravity. As explained in *The Telling* (p. 200), the authors of the Haggadah included it for two reasons:

a. To teach us the nature of freedom

b. To help us evaluate moments in our lives

The passage teaches us that freedom, properly exercised, is not an accomplishment to be celebrated. It is an opportunity that needs a purpose. Per the eighteenth-century British political philosopher Edmund Burke: "The effect of liberty to individuals is that they might do what they please. We ought to see what it will please them to do before we risk congratulations."

1. What do you do with your many freedoms? What might you do with these freedoms to contribute to the world?

_____

_____

_____

_____

_____

_____

_____

2. Where else in your life, aside from the consideration of freedom, might you need to be careful about risking congratulations? Where might you make the strategic mistake of saying "Mission Accomplished" when the task is ongoing, or just beginning?

_____

_____

_____

_____

_____

_____

Our Pesach celebration helps us identify those responsibilities and provides us with the infrastructure to fulfill them in accordance with our ideals and our potential. Our genuine freedom is the ability to make it worthy of celebration.

—*THE TELLING, P. 202*

WHY DID GOD WAIT? WHEN BAD THINGS HAPPEN TO GOOD PEOPLE

The Egyptians did evil to us and afflicted us.

The slavery in Egypt existed for many years. Why did God allow it? Why, for that matter, does God allow slavery anywhere in his world—in the past or in the present? By extension, why does God, who is omnipotent, permit evil? This is the fundamental question of theodicy, and it is often asked in combination with another perennial theological question: How could God be omnipotent while simultaneously granting us free will?

As *The Telling* explains (pp. 203–205), these two questions have the same answer. One way God exercises his omnipotence is by relinquishing some of his power, never to be able to capture it again. This is what God did when he granted people free will. However, people, being the fallible beings that we are, inevitably act outside the dictates of God's will. And this is what causes suffering. Human suffering, thus, is the inevitable casualty of free will.

But this doesn't explain why thousands of people die in natural disasters or pandemics.

To explain this requires a dose of humility and linguistic precision—not to mention, as we've seen before, asking the right question. The Hebrew language has two words for "why": *madua* and *lama*.

Madua seeks to explain what the *Hebrew Language Detective* calls "the cause of a past occurrence," as in: "Why did the item that dropped from the table fall to the ground?"

Lama seeks to explain "toward what end," as in: "Why did you behave that way?"

When the parent of a child who died of cancer works to cure that cancer or comfort families in similar situations, or when a famous athlete writes about his depression to make it socially acceptable for others suffering from mental illness to acknowledge theirs, they are constructing an answer to the *lama*.

When asking *why* a bad thing happened, we must recognize that our human minds cannot comprehend the *madua*: the cause. But we can seek to understand the *lama*: the purpose.

1. For what in your life do you try to find the *madua*?

2. How does the answer change if you ask *lama*?

> We can scientifically explain why a ball thrown in the air comes down, but not why a bad thing happened to a good person. But asking the *lama* question—asking to what end something bad happened—presents an opportunity.
>
> —*THE TELLING*, P. 205

JEW HATRED, EXPLAINED

The Egyptians did evil to us—as it says: Let us deal
with them wisely lest they multiply and, if we happen to
be at war they might join our enemies and fight against us.
And they afflicted us—as it says: They set taskmasters over
them in order to oppress them with their burdens; and they
built Pithom and Raamses as treasure cities for Pharaoh.
They imposed hard labor upon us.

Why do Jew haters hate us, and what can we do about it? In Exodus 1:7–12, we see the birth not only of Jew hatred but of the Jewish people itself. They were not a people or a nation yet, but a family: the Children of Israel. The Pharaoh's concern was that this family would multiply quickly, and by virtue of that expansion subvert the Pharaoh's power. So the Pharaoh simultaneously invented the Jewish people and Jew hatred.

And this is the lesson of Jew hatred. Jew hatred has nothing to do with Jews. The Pharaoh became a Jew hater by associating the Jew with the destruction of the thing most precious to him: the preservation of his regime. In seemingly every case of Jew hatred since, the Jew hater has also associated the Jew with the opposite of the thing most sacred to him. The hatred grows out of the fears of the hater rather than anything inherent in the hated. And for that reason, there is precious little that the Jews can do to change the Jew hater's mind.

1. Think about an example of Jew hatred that you have experienced or witnessed. What is its obvious flaw—its apparent ridiculousness?

_____

_____

_____

_____

_____

_____

_____

_____

_____

_____

_____

_____

_____

_____

_____

_____

_____

_____

_____

> Today, Jew haters with any sophistication say that they are fine with Jews, speak warmly of Jewish friends, and even drop a phrase in Hebrew—and work to delegitimize, weaken, or destroy the country where more than half of the world's Jews live and where the Jewish dream is being lived.
>
> —*THE TELLING,* P. 210

THE PRAYER

We cried out to Hashem, the God of our fathers—as it says:
It happened in the course of those many days that the king of
Egypt died; and the Children of Israel groaned because of their
servitude and cried; their cry because of the servitude rose
up to God. Hashem heard our cry.

In this brief description, the authors of the Haggadah highlight for us the Jewish conception of prayer, and how it is founded on two interrelated principles.

The first is that prayer is not *transactional,* but *relational.* The name used for Hashem when he heard our cry in this context is the one that represents the attribute of mercy or, you might say, intimacy. This is the same name for God in the common formula for Hebrew blessings: *Baruch Ata Hashem,* Blessed are You, Hashem. The inclusion of "you" in the context of blessing signifies the personal, intimate relationship between the person and God. This "you," per Rabbi David Wolpe, is only used to address someone who is "right there."

When we speak to God in this way, we are addressing someone who is physically right beside us—connoting a familiarity and an intimacy that can only be experienced in the context of a committed relationship.

As explained in *The Telling* (p. 218), it thus makes sense that the Hebrew word for "to pray" is *lehitpalel,* a reflexive verb. By praying to God, we are fundamentally changing ourselves.

The relational quality of Jewish prayer does not exist solely in the relationship between man and God. It is about the relationship of the individual to the community as well: "*We* cried out to Hashem . . . Hashem heard *our* cry." Jewish prayer both requires and builds community. It is for this reason that we pray in a minyan.

And "our cry" is literal, audible. We do not pray in our minds or our hearts, but in our lips. The Yiddish word for "to pray," *daven,* is to move one's lips.

So when we pray in Judaism, we are speaking communally, and with one another, for one another. It reminds us to match our supplications with those of the community.

1. What do you pray for?

_____
_____
_____
_____
_____
_____

2. Who do you pray for?

_____
_____
_____
_____
_____
_____

3. How have your prayers changed you?

_____
_____
_____
_____

> God is not an ATM whose bounty can be unlocked with the right code, a pharmacist who can dispense a drug that will make the problem all better, or a DJ who will play a request if asked nicely.
>
> —*THE TELLING*, P. 217

WHAT IT MEANS TO KNOW

God remembered His covenant with Abraham, with Isaac, and with Jacob. God saw the Children of Israel and God knew.

The Torah often says, "God remembered." Could this mean that God might have forgotten—and, at least temporarily, not known something?

For example, the Torah tells us that God "remembered" Noah in the ark. Does this mean that God said, outside of the text, "Oh, yeah—Noah! The guy I told to build the ark while I destroyed the world in a flood. He's still floating around?"

No. That would be inconceivable. What, then, could "remember" mean? Whenever the Torah tells us that someone "remembered," it is a prelude to action. Mere cognitive awareness is never dignified by it being considered "knowledge." If we are aware of something and don't act on it, the Torah is telling us that it is as though we never "knew" it.

1. What do you "remember" in the modern sense—but not in the Torah's sense? What, in other words, are you "aware" of but not acting on sufficiently?

_____

_____

_____

_____

_____

_____

_____

_____

_____

_____

_____

_____

_____

_____

_____

_____

_____

_____

_____

_____

> "Repentance," regardless of how strongly it is "felt," does not exist without confession and restitution. If one knows something but does not act accordingly, it is as if he was never aware of it.
>
> —*THE TELLING*, P. 224

THE UNFINISHED: THE JEWISH WAY OF LIFE AND DEATH

He brought us to this place, and He gave us this Land,
a Land flowing with milk and honey.

—This is not in the Haggadah (Let's see why!)

It is curious that the Haggadah, the story of Jewish redemption, doesn't conclude with the arrival of the Jewish people in the Land of Israel. The omission is glaring throughout. For instance, we read in the Haggadah of the covenant that God made with Abraham in Genesis 15:13–14: "Know well that your offspring shall be strangers in a land not theirs, and they shall be enslaved and oppressed for four hundred years. But I will execute judgment on the nation they shall serve, and in the end they shall go free with great wealth." But the Haggadah omits the subsequent passage "your descendants will return here to this Land."

Far from acknowledging the Jews' eventual arrival in the Promised Land, the Haggadah has us wishing to be in the Holy Land *next* year! Why?

Judaism is not about endings but about continuation. This is true even when it comes to life and death. The Torah portions that relate the deaths of Sarah and Jacob are referred to as, respectively, Chaye Sarah ("Life of Sarah") and Vayechi ("And he [Jacob] lived").

What are the practical implications for us to practice a faith in which the important things never end? It tells us what a full Jewish life is. It is one where we set, and insistently work toward, a goal that we cannot achieve in our lifetime.

The purpose of the Haggadah, and of Judaism in general, is to accentuate the unfinished nature of our work in partnership with God to improve the world.

1. What is your Jewish goal—the one (or two) that you will work insistently to achieve but will not be able to complete in your lifetime?

What is a full Jewish life? It is one that does not end.

—*THE TELLING*, P. 232

WHY JEWISH BOYS EMERGE FROM THE WOMB UNCIRCUMCISED

Take this staff in your hand, that you may perform miracles with it.

When God told Moses, "Take your staff" in Exodus 7:9, what was he really saying? God could have enabled Moses to perform miracles and initiate the plagues with any tool he wished, or no tool at all. So why the staff?

Much would later be done with this staff, beginning with turning it into a snake, then using it to turn water to blood in the first plague, make Egypt teem with frogs, part the Red Sea, and win the battle against the Amalekites.

The staff was therefore tantamount to Moses's God-given gifts and abilities. But the Torah makes an interesting point in Exodus 17. God commanded Moses, "Pass before the people and take with you some of the elders of Israel; and take in your hand *your staff* with which you struck the Nile [to create blood with the first plague]." The next reference to the staff comes only four verses later when Moses tells the people how they are going to win the battle against the attacking Amalekites: "Tomorrow I will stand on top of the hill with the *staff of God* in my hands."

So whose staff was it? When Moses spoke, he said that it was God's. When God spoke, he said that it belonged to Moses.

The answer, of course, is that it belonged to both. God gives us tools so that they may be used in partnership with God. God has always worked with partners. In Genesis 1:26 when God said, "Let us make man," who was the "us"? Every mother who has sung a song to her unborn child will understand. He was speaking with the humanity he was about to birth.

The reason God commanded Moses to use his staff in performing his miracles was to illustrate that each and every one of us has a staff, a God-given gift that we are to use in our partnership with him. But the lesson of the staff is that it must be used in accordance with God's will, not against God's wishes, as when Moses used the staff to strike the rock rather than speak to it in Numbers 20.

1. What are two of your personal staffs?

_____

_____

_____

_____

_____

_____

_____

_____

_____

2. How have you used them in the past to partner with God? How can you use them in the coming year?

_____

_____

_____

_____

_____

_____

_____

_____

_____

> The consistent prominence of this piece of used equipment at many of the pivotal moments in the Torah guides us to one of the fundamental principles of Judaism.
>
> —*THE TELLING*, P. 238

WHY ANY PLAGUES?

Although Seder goers are very familiar with the plagues and their increasing severity, if we take a step back to ask why God sent the plagues, we may be left with a confounding answer. If the purpose was to free the Jews, why was all the violence necessary?

An omnipotent God could have used all sorts of methods to free the Jews. Given a couple minutes to think of some nonviolent alternatives, anyone at your Seder could likely come up with at least two or three ideas. A magic carpet that flies Jews from Egypt to the desert would be one. A giant water slide that starts in Egypt and ends in the desert would be another.

But much like Jew hatred, the plagues weren't really about the Jews per se. The purpose of the plagues, as explained in *The Telling* (p. 241), was to demonstrate God's power to the Egyptians, to convince the most powerful regime in the ancient world that he is the one true God. In that sense, it was part of the debate between slaveholding polytheism and ethical monotheism.

1. How might God have freed the Jews without the plagues? (Remember: God is all powerful—be creative! Ask the children first to get those creative juices flowing.)

2. What might God be trying to teach you?

3. How might God be doing so?

> Who is Hashem that I should heed His voice to send out Israel? I do not know Hashem.
>
> —THE PHARAOH

FIRST, HARMLESS MAGIC

Before initiating any plagues, God instructed Moses and Aaron to perform the kind of magic to which the Pharaoh and his court magicians would be accustomed—the turning of the staff into a snake.

Snake tricks were common in ancient Egypt, and are now easily understood. The Egyptian cobra can be immobilized but not killed by squeezing its neck at a particular place. It could then be placed into a rod. When the rod is thrown to the ground, the snake comes out. And there are other techniques for this trick as well.

What was unique in this case was what happened next. Aaron's staff swallowed the Egyptian staffs. This was different. The Egyptian magicians were accustomed to staffs swallowing snakes, but not other staffs.

But such a marvel did not impress the Pharaoh as much as embolden him. The Pharaoh's heart, we are told, became hardened. God's attempt at a peaceful display of his mastery over Egyptian religion—the magic trick—may have succeeded technically. But it failed strategically.

1. Why would the Pharaoh's reaction be not awe but stubbornness?

2. When in your life have you reacted with stubbornness?

Why would God pick a test that the Egyptians could easily emulate, especially as the Pharaoh could have interpreted it as vindicating his god?

—*THE TELLING*, P. 243

RATIONALITY: FIGHTING BLOOD, FROGS, AND LICE WITH . . . MORE BLOOD, FROGS, AND LICE

It may not be strange that the Pharaoh's magicians attempted to match Aaron's trick of turning the staff into a snake. What is strange is that they continued trying to match Moses's supernatural acts, not only delightful miracles or illusions, but the plagues as well. When Moses turned the Nile to blood, "the Egyptian magicians did the same with their spells" and when the land teemed with frogs, "the magicians did the same with their spells, and brought frogs upon the land of Egypt." For the plague of gnats, his magicians tried (and failed) to make more gnats.

But why? As the leader of the society, ought the Pharaoh have tried to save his people rather than replicate, and thus exacerbate, the catastrophe?

He should have, but he didn't. Why not? Because he hated the Jews. The Pharaoh's actions in the story exemplify the logic of the Jew hatred that he invented. For instance, many people today say that a nuclear Iran would not attack Israel because Israel's inevitable second strike would be devastating. No Iranian leader would put his people in such danger. But that is not the logic of former Iranian president Akbar Hashemi Rafsanjani, as articulated in his 2001 "Jerusalem Day" address: "If one day the Islamic world is equipped with weapons like those Israel possesses now, then the imperialist strategy will reach a standstill because even the use of one nuclear bomb within Israel will destroy everything. However, it will only harm the Islamic world. It is not irrational to contemplate such an eventuality."

The ideology of Jew hatred, lived by Jew haters throughout history (as explained in *The Telling*, p. 207), is simple. The notion of rationality derives from the value of the outcome. Is it rational for Jew haters to suffer considerably in order to maximally harm the Jew? As Jew haters from the Pharaoh on have consistently demonstrated, yes.

The antithesis of all-consuming hatred is immense gratitude. And that is what this story is actually about. Rashi observes that God told Moses *to tell Aaron* to strike either the water or the earth to produce each of these three plagues: blood, frogs, gnats.

Why the circuitous action? Because Moses was obliged to show gratitude to the water, for it was the waters of the Nile that carried him to safety as a baby, and it was the earth that accepted the corpse of the Egyptian man he killed in defense of the Jewish man whom the Egyptian was attacking. If Moses owed gratitude to the inanimate, how much gratitude must we owe to the living beings around us?

1. What are some objectives for which you'd spend (or do) a lot that might appear (to others) to contradict your self-interest?

_____

_____

_____

_____

2. To whom should you show more gratitude?

_____

_____

_____

> Here, the Pharaoh, intent on enslaving the Jews and defeating their God, *thoughtfully and purposefully* increases the amount of blood and frogs that are defiling and destroying Egypt.
> It is just a price the Egyptians are willing to pay to afflict the Jews and their God.
>
> —*THE TELLING*, PP. 245–246

HABITS: HOW THE PHARAOH TEACHES US TO LIVE FREELY

One of the most common questions related to the story of the Exodus relates to the hardening of the Pharaoh's heart. How was the Pharaoh to be held responsible for his decisions if his "heart was hardened"?

The answer comes, as it often does in Judaism, and in life, by asking the right question. Who did the hardening? A careful reading of the text reveals that God only stepped in to harden the Pharaoh's heart after the sixth plague, boils. During the first five plagues, the Pharaoh hardened his own heart.

This reveals a basic yet counterintuitive human truth. We tend to think that our conscious psychology precedes human action—we develop a conviction or a feeling and then act accordingly. In fact, the opposite is true. We are the sum of our habits. Our actions determine our thoughts, and the combination of actions and thoughts determines who we are.

In the Talmud, there is a debate among several leading rabbis over the most important passage in the Torah. Several rabbis propose possibilities from the creation story in Genesis to the declaration of the oneness of God in the Shema. But the victor in this debate is Rabbi Shimon ben Pazi, who chooses the apparently pedestrian verse from Exodus 29:39: "The first lamb you shall sacrifice in the morning and the second lamb you shall sacrifice in the evening."

Rabbi Shimon ben Pazi's point is the value of consistency. The habits we choose further determine the way we live and the choices we make.

The Pharaoh had made a habit of his hard heart, and it was that self-hardening that ultimately curtailed his free will. The lesson to us is clear. If you want to change who you are, make a habit of doing the things you want to be. How long will it take? In the Talmud, Rabbi Yochanan said that it takes thirty days. A 2009 study from the *European Journal of Social Psychology* reported that the formation of a habit takes an average of sixty-six days.

The first day can be today.

1. What one additional characteristic would you like to add in the coming three months?

_____

_____

_____

_____

_____

_____

_____

2. What habit will you adopt to embody that characteristic—starting tomorrow, and continuing every day thereafter?

_____

_____

_____

_____

_____

_____

> The Jewish philosophy of habit is embodied in the magnificent expression *second nature*. While the idea of one's nature might be complicated (from what it is to how to modify it), one's second nature is very real and not at all complicated. And neither, *thrillingly*, is changing it.
>
> —*THE TELLING*, P. 251

"ALL MY PLAGUES": THE ESSENCE OF GOD, REVEALED IN HAIL

By the seventh plague, God had issued an ultimatum. The Pharaoh was given the opportunity to acknowledge God, and if he refused, the next plague—"a very heavy hail at this time tomorrow, the likes of which have never occurred in Egypt from the day it was founded until now"—would come.

The ultimatum even came with a warning: "Now, gather in your livestock and all that you have in the field. The hail shall fall on any man or beast that is found in the field and not brought into the house, and they will die."

What is the purpose of a warning? Are warnings issued by those who want to inflict maximum harm, or prevent that harm from occurring in the first place? In combat, warnings can be a disastrous tactic if the purpose is to win a fight. A warning lets your opponent know what you have planned. The only reason to issue it is to avoid executing the plan.

This reminds us that the purpose of the plagues was not to free the Jews, but to win an argument. The plagues were a display of Hashem's power and existence as the one true God. By issuing the warning to prevent harm, God was saying, "I am your God, too. In fact, I'm everyone's God and there is none other."

The Torah tells us in Exodus 9:20 that some people heeded the warning. "Whoever feared the word of God among Pharaoh's servants drove his servants and his livestock into the houses." Others did not. "But whoever did not put his heart to the word of God left his servants and his livestock in the field."

But after seven plagues, why didn't *all* the Egyptians heed the warning?

Rabbi Norman Lamm, in a sermon from 1955, noted how the Torah describes the two classes of Egyptians. There were those who "feared the word of God" and took shelter. And there were those who "did not put his heart to the word of God." Rabbi Lamm pointed out that these two are not natural opposites. The natural opposite of one who does not fear God is one who does not believe in God or one who rejects God. So why does the Torah present indifference to God as the opposite of fearing him?

The Torah is teaching us that when it comes to God, apathy is worse than ignorance or disbelief. A casual relationship with God is the antithesis of divine relationality.

1. When have you been indifferent to God or anyone (or anything) important to you?

_____

_____

_____

_____

_____

_____

_____

_____

2. How have you experienced or observed warnings as being acts of compassion and love?

_____

_____

_____

_____

_____

_____

_____

_____

The Torah . . . casts indifference to God as the opposite
of fearing him.

—THE TELLING, P. 253

"CAN'T YOU SEE EGYPT IS LOST?": WHEN CHANGE IS HARDER THAN IT SHOULD BE

After seven plagues, God realized that he was no closer to convincing the Pharaoh of his power and dominion. What follows is a divine lesson in how to deal with failure.

The first step was for God to recognize the situation for what it was. Unable to persuade the Egyptians, God pivoted. No longer interested in convincing the Egyptians, his goal shifted to sending his message through the Jewish people, rather than winning over the other nations of the world directly.

In this sequence of events, we realize that the God of the Torah is a learning God. Unlike the Pharaoh, whose heart weakened and hardened over the course of plagues, never changing his pattern of reaction, God learns from the past. In the story of the Exodus he shifted to a more achievable goal than he had previously envisioned.

1. When in the past year have you needed to shift goals when one wasn't working out? What are your reflections on the experience?

2. Are you working toward a goal right now that could use shifting?

3. Have you, or has anyone you know, ever persisted in an obviously wrong position? Why do you think the false belief persisted?

> How long will this one be a stumbling block to us? Let the people go and they will worship their God. Do you not yet know that Egypt is lost?
>
> —THE PHARAOH'S SERVANTS

THE NINTH PLAGUE: WHEN EVEN LIGHTING A CANDLE, TO SAVE MY LIFE, IS IMPOSSIBLE

If we accept the common understanding that the plagues increase in severity, why would the ninth plague, darkness, be worse than boils, pestilence, and economy-destroying locusts?

At first glance, it may seem that this plague was perhaps even less severe than many that preceded it. But a careful reading of the Torah's description leads to a different interpretation. This plague is described in Exodus 10:22 as a "thick darkness" so powerful that "no person could see his brother, nor could any person rise from his place for three days." The Egyptians, it would seem, had an easy solution. According to the National Candle Association, candles were invented five thousand years ago, millennia before the Exodus—in Egypt. The Egyptians could have avoided or mitigated this plague by lighting a candle. Why didn't they?

The darkness of the ninth plague was not simply a lack of actual light. Darkness instills fear, and fear can be paralyzing. A person in fear, as explained in *The Telling* (p. 258), becomes immobilized and incapable of trusting anyone. Without the ability to trust, the victims of this plague cannot form relationships with anyone, including close family. That is why the Torah says that no man could "see his brother" . . . not that no man could see "another."

With the fear produced by darkness, even this most basic of relationships—brotherhood—is impossible. And without relationships, as explained in *The Telling* (p. 259), one will become vulnerable to the debilitating mental illness of depression. And that is what this plague is, an epidemic of depression in a defeated society.

1. How might you identify someone who is depressed, or heading toward depression, and help them before they are effectively immobilized?

_____

_____

_____

_____

_____

_____

_____

_____

_____

_____

_____

_____

_____

_____

_____

> I know I am perplexed that my fears are irrational, incoherent. At times I am given over to panic; I am afraid of death . . . I don't know what to fear, what not to fear; I am utterly confused and ignorant. Modern man is, existentially, a slave because he is ignorant and fails to identify his own needs [regarding what to fear].
>
> —RABBI JOSEPH B. SOLOVEITCHIK

PRELUDE TO THE TENTH PLAGUE: MOSES BECOMES A LEADER

The tenth plague was the most severe of the plagues. As described by Moses in Exodus 11:4:

> Toward midnight I will go forth among the Egyptians, and every firstborn in the land of Egypt shall die, from the firstborn of Pharaoh who sits on his throne to the firstborn of the slave girl who is behind the millstones and all the firstborn of the cattle. And there will be a great cry in all the land of Egypt, that there has been none like it and there won't continue to be like it. But not a dog will move its tongue at any of the Children of Israel, from man to animal, so that you'll know that God will distinguish between Egypt and Israel. And all these servants of yours will come down to me, and they'll bow to me, saying: "Go out, you and all the people who are at your feet." And after that, I'll go out!

We are told that Moses left the Pharaoh's presence "in burning anger" and it is in this anger that we can see Moses's leadership on display. Unlike a shallow, self-absorbed anger, the anger of Moses in this context was righteous, one of indignation. Having told the Pharaoh that at about midnight, God will strike down the Egyptian firstborn, Moses had hoped that the Pharaoh would do something to stop it. But this is not what the Pharaoh chose. Resh Lakish, the rabbi in the Talmud who was previously a gladiator, imagines Moses slapping the Pharaoh in the face, as if to try literally to knock sense into him—and avoid the killings that are otherwise going to happen.

This teaches us the difference between a righteous anger and gratuitous anger. Gratuitous anger is the anger of a petty tyrant. Moses's anger was out of concern for Pharaoh's people. It was a righteous anger—a leader's anger, a teacher's anger.

1. What, in your life, might be worthy of righteous anger?

2. When is your anger unrighteous?

Maimonides . . . likens anger to idolatry and states that it causes wisdom to depart from a scholar and the prophetic spirit to depart from a prophet.

—*THE TELLING, P. 261*

ALLEGIANCES BUILD: THE ARCHITECTURE OF RELATIONSHIPS, THE CONSTITUTION OF SOCIETY

Per Exodus 12:3, there were to be "no leftovers" from the first Passover meal. It takes at least fifteen people to consume a lamb. No household could do so alone. Hence, the Torah's message was that the first, and fundamental, act of a free people was to give and share—and, in so doing, to create a community.

Community is the bedrock of Jewish life and cultural transmission. And the community requires each and every person. "Each" man was to take a lamb for his household. Individuals could participate differently, as hosts or attendees, but the governing principle of the arrangement remained the same: community.

As stated in *The Telling* (p. 266), strong individuals create good families. Good families provide the bulwark for vibrant communities. Vibrant communities create healthy societies. Healthy societies enable great nations. And great nations inspire the world. It is through building strong families and communities that universalist values can be effectively taught and enacted.

1. What are the important allegiances and associations that you have?

2. When you think of the community organizations that are most important to you, what kind of people are the most dependable, enthusiastic, and effective contributors?

> To be attached to the subdivision, to love the little platoon we belong to in society, is the first principle (the germ as it were) of public affections. It is the first link in the series by which we proceed towards a love of our country, and to mankind.
>
> —EDMUND BURKE

HASTE: THE MORAL IMPERATIVE OF SPEED

In Exodus 12:11, the Torah stipulates that the Pesach meal be eaten "in haste."

This is not the only instance of haste in the Torah. In Genesis 18, we are told of three strangers who visited Abraham's tent as he was recovering from his circumcision. In the midst of what was likely a painful recuperation, Abraham "hurried" to Sarah to "quick" make some cakes, before he "ran" to select a calf for his servant, who "hurried" to prepare it.

Many years later, Rebecca "quickly lowered" the jug for Abraham's servant, and then "hurried and emptied her jug into the trough and kept running to the well to draw water" for the camels.

Speed in the fulfilment of deeds is a great value in the Torah. The deeds of the righteous are done in haste. As explained in *The Telling* (p. 270), if one waits, the deed may never get done. An alliance between rationalization, deprioritization, and forgetfulness is always ready to do battle, often secretly, against the urge to do a good deed—and will usually win.

1. When you think of a good deed to do, how quickly do you usually do it?

2. When you delay doing the good deed, how often do you actually get around to doing it?

3. What good deeds will you do faster in the coming year?

4. What good deed can you do right now, today?

> When the time of its performance [that of a good deed] comes, or when it happens to present itself to him, or when the thought of performing it enters his mind, he should hurry and hasten to seize hold of it and perform it, and not allow time to lapse.
>
> —RABBI MOSES CHAIM LUZZATTO

THE TENTH PLAGUE: WHAT IT MEANS THAT THE JEWS ARE THE CHOSEN PEOPLE

Toward midnight I will go forth among the Egyptians, and every firstborn in the land of Egypt shall die, from the firstborn of Pharaoh who sits on his throne to the firstborn of the slave girl who is behind the millstones and all the firstborn of the cattle. And there will be a big cry in all the land of Egypt, that there has been none like it and there won't continue to be like it.

The slaying of the firstborn is one of the most commonly misunderstood events in the Torah. The prevailing interpretation of this plague is literal, that the firstborn child of every household will be killed.

But what is the biblical meaning of the word *firstborn*? In Exodus 4:22, God commanded Moses, "Say to Pharaoh, 'So said Hashem, my firstborn son is Israel.'" But even the Torah itself doesn't claim that the Jews were the first people. Abraham, the first Jew, fought in a war involving nine other peoples. And those didn't include the Amorites, the Canaanites, the Hittites, the Perizzites, the Jebusites, and others.

In the language of the Torah, "firstborn" is not about chronology. It is about transmission. The firstborn of a household yields tremendous influence over the younger children, and is therefore crucial to the transmission of the parents' values. The firstborn is thus the culture carrier, the transmitter of cultural values. In telling Moses to tell the Pharaoh that the Jews are his firstborn, God wanted the Pharaoh to know that the Jews were the people to transmit the message of ethical monotheism to the nations of the world.

The slaying of the Egyptian firstborn was thus not a literal killing of the oldest child of every household. Rather, those who upheld and sought to transmit Egypt's slaveholding, polytheistic culture, were cut down. This was God's way of ensuring that such a culture, that drowned all Jewish baby boys in the Nile, would be destroyed.

1. Who are the carriers of our culture?

2. Who ought to be the carriers of our culture?

3. How can you be a better carrier of your culture?

> We are to be God's culture carriers, the people who transmit the message of ethical monotheism to the nations of the world.
>
> —*THE TELLING*, P. 273

HOVERING, RESCUING, AND PROTECTING: NO ONE "PASSED OVER" ANYTHING, AND WHY THAT IS IMPORTANT

The English term *Passover* is, simply, a misnomer. As the Torah tells us in Exodus 12:23, God sent the "destroyer" to slay the Egyptian firstborn. In that circumstance, what did we want God to do? To "pass over" our homes? Absolutely not! We wanted him to do just about anything else—particularly to hover over, to protect, and to guard us.

And that's exactly what the word *pesach*—mistranslated as "Passover"—means. We know this from the reference to the word *pasach* in Isaiah 31:5: "Like birds hovering overhead / the Lord Almighty will shield it and deliver it / He will *pasach* it and will rescue it."

When God was "hovering over" our homes, protecting us in order to rescue us, he was also doing something else. He was preparing us for a new kind of relationship, an intimate and loving relationship.

Far from passing over us, God was watching over us.

If "Passover" is a complete misnomer, some might ask, why then would God have had us put blood on our doorposts immediately before the tenth plague? It is commonly (and incorrectly) thought that we placed the blood on the doorposts in order to identify our homes as Jewish so God would "pass over" them. But God had already exempted Jewish homes before, without having us mark them. He presumably did not lose the capability of identifying the Jewish homes before the final plague.

Why, then, would God have had us mark the doorposts of our homes with blood? As Rabbi Norman Lamm explained, we did not do that for God—but for us. We marked our doorposts—the liminal space of the home—in order to remind ourselves, when we leave and when we arrive, that we do so as Jews.

1. How can you be a better Jew out of the house?

_____

_____

_____

_____

_____

_____

2. How can you be a better Jew inside the house?

_____

_____

_____

_____

_____

_____

3. How can you be a better person inside/outside the house?

_____

_____

_____

_____

_____

> On the most important night in history, God is telling us: You must be a Jew in your comings and your goings. You must be a Jew when you are at home and when you are in the world.
>
> —*THE TELLING, P. 277*

WATCHING: THE EXISTENTIAL EXPERIENCE

As explained in *The Telling* (p. 280), there are two ways to watch a person or a group: as a mechanism for evaluation or as an expression of caring. On the night of our last meal in Egypt, we went from being watched by malevolent slave masters to being watched by a benevolent God.

This new experience of watching would become a motif for the most profound love of all time. As George and Ira Gershwin wrote in 1926, "There is someone I am longing to see / I hope that he turns out to be / Someone to watch over me." Parents watch over their children's cribs, and children watch over their parents at the end of life. What do these parents say in those final moments? "Promise me that you will watch over your mother (or brother or sister) when I'm gone."

1. Who has watched over you in the past year?

2. Who will you watch over in the coming year?

3. Who do you want watching over whom when your days are done?

What do we want the person doing the watching (ourselves, our child's spouse, the person we are asking on our deathbed) to watch for? Anything and everything, always and forever— whatever, at any given point, our beloved needs to be shielded, protected, and rescued from.

—*THE TELLING*, P. 281

WHY POLITICAL ARGUMENTS ARE USUALLY A WASTE OF TIME, OR WORSE

The plagues didn't work. When the Jews left, the Pharaoh sent "all the chariots of Egypt" to catch us and bring us back to servitude.

Why did this show of force and words fail so completely? The Pharaoh simply could not accept anything outside of his own belief. As described in *The Telling* (p. 283), social scientists today have demonstrated that the parts of our brain that are associated with pleasure are aroused when our views are confirmed.

Even the Jews themselves, freed by God from an oppressive slavery, soon turned on that very God and complained about their situation in the desert, being fed heavenly manna and protected by divine clouds. Not only did the plagues fail to win over the Egyptians, they seem also to have failed to win over the Jews.

We learn, as did God, a powerful lesson from this. Spectacular gestures and ecstatic moments rarely lead to sustained change. Such change almost always comes as a result of long-term commitment, of genuine compassion (actual "suffering with"), of demonstrated respect and acts of love.

The Exodus was just the beginning of the process of showing even the Jews the glory of God. The lesson, as Rabbi David Wolpe says, is that this kind of education would "have to be done in every generation and with every child." Hence, the Seder.

1. Have you ever changed your mind about a deeply held belief? How did it happen?

2. Are there beliefs you hold on to today, in the midst of overwhelming evidence to the contrary?

> The Books of Exodus and Numbers are basically chronicles of Jewish intransigence, rebellion, and insecurity that manifest (multiple times) in a stated desire to go back to Egypt! So the plagues don't work with the Egyptians and don't even work when redirected to convince the Jews.
>
> —*THE TELLING*, P. 284

THE SECRET TO HAPPINESS AND GOODNESS

Rabbi Jose the Galilean said: How does one derive that the Egyptians . . . were struck by fifty plagues and at the Sea by two hundred and fifty!

Why does the Haggadah relate to us a plague-counting contest? And how is it that the range is so vast, from sixty to three hundred—a 500 percent variation?

The high numbers indicate to us that Rabbis Jose the Galilean, Eliezer, and Akiva were counting more than the plagues per se. These rabbis must have been defining divine interventions (or miracles) as plagues. It is thus an invitation for us to discuss and understand the nature of miracles.

So, what is a miracle? The *Oxford Dictionary of Phrase and Fable*'s definition of a miracle is: "A surprising and welcome event that is not explicable by natural and scientific laws and is therefore considered to be the work of a divine agency."

The Jewish understanding of miracles is exactly the opposite. Miracles abound. It is not merely the child who survives a devastating disease against all odds. It is also the child who gets well from a basic over-the-counter treatment, and the child who never gets sick at all.

The rabbis' plague-counting contest was actually a miracle-counting contest, and illustrates to us how many miracles we can witness every day if we open our eyes to them. In this clever way, the Haggadah is calling upon us to do so.

The Telling shows (p. 290) how modern social science has verified that our happiness is contingent upon our miracle identification skills. To the extent that we regard a child's laugh, the rising sun, in the love we feel, the functioning of any of the technologies that make our lives easier possible, as miraculous—we will be happier. As Rabbi Abraham Joshua Heschel wrote, "wonder and amazement" constitute "the chief characteristic of the religious man's attitude toward history and nature."

1. Start in the morning, and equip yourself with a note-taking device. Identify as many miracles as you can throughout the day. How many miracles did you identify?

2. How do you feel after having done so?

> Every day, miracles befall a person as great as the miracles of the Exodus.
>
> **—TANNA D'VEI ELIYAHU**

"DAYENU": HOW TO EXPRESS GRATITUDE

We learn from Rabbis Jose the Galilean, Eliezer, and especially Akiva why we should count many miracles, and the song "Dayenu" (*It Would Have Been Enough*) shows us how we should do so. When one realizes just how many miracles occur on a daily basis, such a realization is bound to spark the most important human emotion: gratitude. And that is what the song "Dayenu" is about.

A striking aspect of this remarkable song is that there are fifteen verses—each articulating a highly specific aspect of the Exodus, all expressing gratitude to God. Why, then, would "Dayenu" not have been one verse: "God—Thanks for Everything"?

Because the song is teaching us how to *express* gratitude. "Dayenu" shows us that everything in a complex system should be regarded as if the whole system depends on it—which it actually does. But even in this irreducible complexity, "Dayenu" teaches us that true gratitude, like love, is always best expressed in the specific. The more specific we are with how we express our thanks, the more deeply it will be appreciated.

1. What are two things that you are grateful for? Follow the chain of events that brought those things into existence. How many people played a role? To how many people are you grateful?

2. How can you best express that gratitude?

Life on earth required God to create the big bang and a perfectly positioned sun, moon, and Jupiter, and lots of other massively improbable events to happen with astonishing precision. If *any* one of them did not happen, there would be no life on earth.

—*THE TELLING*, P. 292

ALWAYS A SECOND CHANCE

What happens if someone misses the Pesach seder? This is not a thought experiment or a hypothetical. It is a question asked and answered in the Torah—and the astonishing answer tells us about the personality of God and how to live well on earth.

This question, asked by ordinary men in the Book of Numbers, is explored in *The Telling* (pp. 294–295). What did God do to address this circumstance? He declared a new holiday—Pesach Sheni (the Second Passover). It is the Jewish holiday and celebration of second chances.

The Jewish God is the God of second chances. We learn, by his example, that we are never out of chances to serve him and improve his world.

1. Are you on a life journey? If so, where are you going?

2. What in your life warrants a second chance?

> Pesach, like everything else meaningfully Jewish, is never finished.
>
> —*THE TELLING*, P. 295

PASSOVER NOTES AND MEMORIES

ABOUT THE AUTHOR

Michael Gerson

MARK GERSON, an entrepreneur and philanthropist, is the co-founder of Gerson Lehrman Group, African Mission Healthcare, and United Hatzalah of Israel. A graduate of Williams College and Yale Law School, Mark is the author of books on intellectual history and education. His articles and essays on subjects ranging from Frank Sinatra to the biblical Jonah have been published in *The New Republic, Commentary, The Wall Street Journal,* and *USA Today.* He hosts the popular podcast *The Rabbi's Husband* and is married to Rabbi Erica Gerson. They and their four children live in New York City.

EXPLORE THE HAGGADAH
IN A POWERFUL NEW WAY WITH
THE TELLING

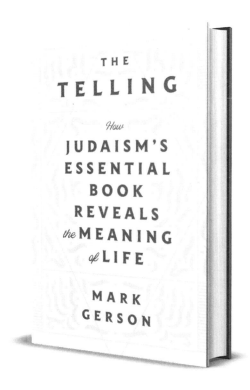